# A POCKET BOOK ON
# DIY

## Mike Lawrence

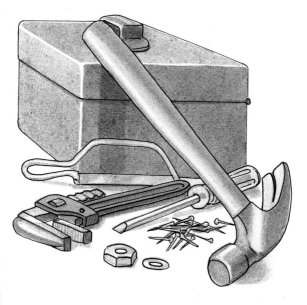

**Editor's note**
Metric and Imperial measurements are given throughout the book, except in the case of materials that are sold either in metric or Imperial units where it is not possible to give accurate conversions.

First published 1984 by
Octopus Books Limited
59 Grosvenor Street
London W1

© 1984 Octopus Books Limited

ISBN 0 7064 2072 1

Produced by Mandarin Publishers Ltd
22a Westlands Road, Quarry Bay, Hong Kong

Illustrations: Josephine Martin of The Garden Studio

# A POCKET BOOK ON
# DIY

More than 100 professional solutions
to home maintenance problems

Mike Lawrence

OCTOPUS BOOKS

## AIRLOCKS

If water will not flow through a pipe, or comes out of a tap in spurts, there is probably an airlock somewhere along the run. It is usually caused by poor plumbing installation, resulting in high spots in the system where air bubbles can collect and interfere with the smooth flow of water. Airlocks can also cause knocking noises in the pipework.

**ACTION**

**1** Check that the affected tap is fed from the hot cylinder or the coldwater storage tank.

**2** Slip a length of garden hose over the affected tap, and secure it with an adjustable clip or stout wire.

**3** Fit the other end of the hose over the kitchen cold tap, which supplies water at mains pressure.

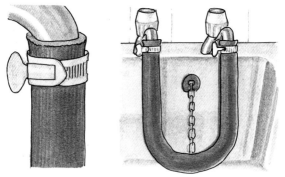

**4** Open the airlocked tap.

**5** Open the kitchen cold tap. The water pressure should force the airlock up through the system to its highest point, so clearing the pipe run. If more than one tap is affected, clear the system from the lowest affected tap.

## ANAGLYPTA

Anaglypta is a trade name that has become a generic term for white wallpaper embossed with a regular design and intended for overpainting. It is ideal for covering less-than-perfect walls and ceilings, and can be redecorated simply by applying a fresh coat of paint over the existing one. However, if you want a complete change of decoration, you are faced with the problem of removing the paper. The same problems apply with other painted wallcoverings.

**ACTION**

**1** Use a knife blade or similar implement to lift a seam or corner of the wallcovering.

**2** Attempt to peel off the wallcovering in complete strips or large pieces, using a flat-bladed scraper to ease difficult areas. This may work if the wall surface beneath was not well prepared originally and adhesion is poor.

**3** If step 2 is wholly or partly successful, soak and scrape off any remaining backing paper from the wall. Add a little washing-up liquid to the warm water to aid its penetration of the paper.

**4** If step 2 fails, you have two choices. The cheap but laborious method is to use a serrated scraper to break up the painted surface; water will then penetrate more easily and allow you to scrape the paper off. The more expensive – but far quicker – method is to hire a steam wallpaper stripper for the day; this works rather like a steam iron, forcing steam into the wallcovering and softening the paste so that large areas can be stripped easily and quickly. It more than repays the hire cost in terms of time saved.

## ARTEX

Artex, like Anaglypta, is a trade name that is now used to describe all textured finishes applied to ceilings (and, less commonly, to walls). Some of these finishes are bought ready-mixed, others as powders that have to be mixed with water. Once applied, they are textured in various ways and left to harden. They can be redecorated by overpainting, but are almost impossible to remove (it will probably be quicker to fit a new plasterboard ceiling).

# ARTEX

## ACTION

**1** To redecorate textured surfaces, first scrub the surface with a soft scrubbing brush and household detergent to remove grease, dirt, etc. Rinse thoroughly.

**2** Allow surface to dry completely, then repaint. A long-pile roller will speed up the work by carrying paint into recesses in the texture more quickly than a brush.

**3** Apply a second coat if coverage is not perfect, or if you are having a major colour change.

**4** Finish off the edges of the textured area neatly with a small brush.

# BALLVALVES

Ballvalves are self-regulating fittings that control the flow of water into cisterns: storage cisterns in the loft and WC cisterns elsewhere in the house. When the cistern is emptied, the float on the ballvalve arm falls with the water level, opening the valve and allowing water to flow into the cistern. When the water reaches the required level, the valve closes again. The valve itself can become corroded or blocked by debris or hard-water scale, and so will not work smoothly. The float can also be affected by corrosion to the point where it is no longer air-tight, so it sinks and causes the valve to malfunction. There are several different patterns of ballvalve, from the older Portsmouth and Croydon types to more modern diaphragm types (often made from plastic rather than brass). There are also two different versions in each case: a high-pressure valve that is fitted to cisterns fed from the rising main; and a low-pressure type used on WC cisterns fed from the storage cistern by water at low pressure. It is important that the right type is used.

## ACTION

**1** If valve is jammed shut or drips constantly, suspect a blockage or internal corrosion. Turn off the water supply to the ballvalve at the appropriate

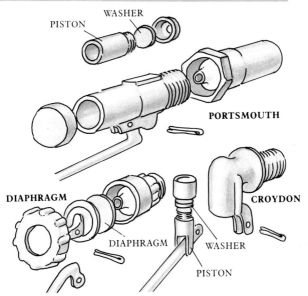

PISTON
WASHER
PORTSMOUTH

DIAPHRAGM
DIAPHRAGM
WASHER
PISTON
CROYDON

stoptap; if one is not fitted on pipe runs to WC cisterns, tie up the ballvalve in the storage cistern feeding it and open the bathroom cold taps to drain the storage cistern.

**2** With a Portsmouth valve (the most common), remove the split pin holding the float arm in place, using pliers.

**3** Unscrew the retaining cap on the end of the valve body (you may need to apply penetrating oil first if it is corroded).

**4** Insert an old screwdriver in the slot on the underside of the valve case and push the piston out.

**5** Unscrew the washer-retaining cap on the end of the piston (grip it with a wrench, and insert a screwdriver in the slot in the piston to stop it turning).

**6** Prise out the old washer and fit a new one, smeared with petroleum jelly.

**7** Replace the washer retaining cap.

**8** Clean up the piston with wire wool or a wire brush, and smear it with petroleum jelly. Clean inside the valve body too.

## BALLVALVES

**9** Turn on water briefly to flush any debris out of the valve. Then replace the piston (washer end first).

**10** Reconnect level arm and restore water supply.

**11** With a Croydon valve, the piston operates vertically rather than horizontally, and is actually attached to the lever arm which is again retained with a split pin. Remove it, replace the washer and reassemble as described.

**12** With a modern diaphragm valve, unscrew the end cap, withdraw the plunger, fit a new rubber diaphragm and reassemble.

**13** If an old ballvalve continues to malfunction, it will be better to replace it entirely with a modern diaphragm type. Unscrew the back-nuts holding the valve to the wall of the cistern, fit the new valve in its place and restore the water supply.

See also CISTERNS, OVERFLOWS and PLUMBING.

## BASINS

The commonest problem with washbasins is blockages: either water flows away very slowly when the plug is pulled out, or the overflow becomes blocked so that the basin itself overflows if the taps are left running inadvertently. The problem is caused by a gradual build-up of scum and hair, either in the trap beneath the basin or in the built-in overflow. However, the remedies are quite simple.

**ACTION**

**1** If the overflow on a ceramic basin is blocked, use bent wire to poke the blockage out via the overflow hole in the basin.

**2** If the blockage clears, flush the overflow through with hot water (pour it into the overflow slot from a kettle, or use a tap-fitting shower hose without the spray head).

**3** If the blockage persists, place a bowl under the trap and dismantle it (leave the plug in and have cloths handy to catch any leaks in confined spaces).

**4** Push wire up the overflow channel from below,

then replace the trap and flush through as before.

**5** On vanity-unit basins with a flexible hose overflow, avoid using wire as you could puncture the hose. Instead, undo the trap beneath the basin, disconnect the overflow hose and flush it through to clear the blockage. Reconnect it.

**6** Check that overflow holes or grilles are clear of scum and hair.

**7** Flush overflows through regularly to prevent scum build-up in the future.

• See also BLOCKAGES and OVERFLOWS.

## BATHS

Apart from blocked outlets and overflows, one of the commonest problems with baths is water getting between the bath and adjacent walls, leading to damaged decorations in rooms below and possibly rot in the floor timbers beneath the bath. The problem is caused by slight movement of the bath when it is in use: the combined weight of bather and water is considerable, and modern plastic baths in particular flex slightly (the problem is less acute with metal baths). As the movement cannot be prevented, filling the gap with anything rigid will not solve the problem; a flexible seal is required so that any movement does not open up fresh gaps.

**ACTION**

**1** If the gap between bath and wall is less than about 3mm (⅛in), it can be filled with special silicone mastic, available in white and many common sanitaryware colours. Clean the bath and wall surface thoroughly with detergent to remove grease and scum.

**2** Cut the nozzle on the mastic tube to give a hole a little wider than the gap.

**3** Pipe a bead of mastic along the gap, paying special attention to corners and any points where the gap widens slightly.

**4** Smooth over the mastic with a moist finger or a length of dowel dipped in water.

**5** Leave until a surface skin has formed, then trim away any excess mastic with a sharp handyman's knife or razor blade.

**6** If the gap is between 3mm (⅛in) and 6mm (¼in), fill the gap first with soft rope, packing it down to 2mm or 3mm (about ⅛in) below the bath rim. Then pipe a wider bead of mastic into place; the rope will stop it from slumping into the gap. Finish off as before.

**7** With very wide or irregular gaps, use special quadrant tiles or painted quadrant beading instead. Pipe non-setting mastic on to the back of the tiles or beading and press into place against the bath rim and wall. Leave the mastic until a surface skin has formed, then trim off any excess.

See also BASINS, BLOCKAGES and OVERFLOWS.

## BELLS

Many door bells and chimes are battery-operated, and are linked to the bellpush with two-core bell wire. Others, especially if they have an illuminated bellpush, are powered from a transformer connected to the mains at a socket outlet or at the consumer unit. If the bell fails to work, flat batteries or a bad connection somewhere on the circuit are the commonest causes. Poor contacts within the bell or chime unit, as a result of condensation and corrosion, can cause irregular ringing.

**ACTION**

**1** If a battery-operated bell will not work, check that the batteries are sitting correctly, in contact with their terminals. Replace them if they are flat.

**2** Check connections within the bell itself, and at the bellpush. Remake them if necessary. With mains-operated bells, check the transformer connections too.

**3** Check that contacts within the bell or chimes are clear of fluff, and clean carefully with fine glasspaper to improve electrical connections.

**4** Check the condition of the bell wire linking the components. If it is damaged or the cores are exposed, fit a new length.

**5** If the bulb in an illuminated bellpush fails, fit a new bulb.

**6** If the bellpush jams when pressed, corrosion may have affected the spring and contact inside. Either open up the push and clean the contacts, or simply replace it with a new one.

## BLOCKAGES

However well-designed and carefully installed your waste system may be, blockages can occur; knowing how to clear them will save a lot of mess and inconvenience. The most common site for a blockage to occur within the house is in the trap fitted beneath every water-using appliance. The purpose of the trap is to stop any smell from gullies and drains entering the house, and its design ensures that the trap itself is always full of water after the appliance has emptied. Modern traps are usually made from plastic, while on old plumbing systems one-piece lead traps may still be found. The trap beneath a WC is a one-piece ceramic casting which cannot be dismantled; with all other traps provision is made for clearing blockages if they occur.

**ACTION**

**1** If water will not run away when a plug is removed, replace the plug and gain access to the trap under the appliance.

**2** With plastic traps, place a bucket or bowl beneath the trap and unscrew the trap from the waste outlet of the appliance. You should be able to do this by hand, but on an obstinate trap use a large adjustable spanner with care.

**3** Unscrew the other end of the trap from the waste run. Take care to retain any washers or O-rings inside the fittings.

**4** Wash and scrub through the trap to remove the blockage. Rinse thoroughly.

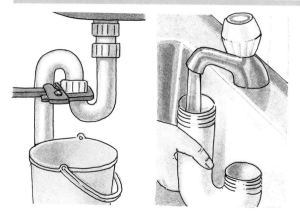

**5** Reassemble the trap, making sure that washers and O-rings are in the right place and are properly seated as you tighten the nuts. Hand pressure should suffice; overtightening can damage the plastic threads. Slight leakage will suggest that the washers are too thin or have perished; fit new ones if this is the case.

**6** Pull out the plug and flush the whole waste run through with plenty of water to ensure that all debris is washed away.

**7** With old-fashioned lead traps, unscrew the cleaning eye in the base of the trap with a spanner. As you do so, brace the trap with a piece of scrap wood so that you do not distort the soft pipework. Make sure you put a bucket underneath the trap, before opening the eye.

**8** Push stiff wire into the trap in both directions to dislodge the blockage.

**9** Flush through trap after replacing cleaning eye.

See also BASINS, DOWNPIPES, DRAINS, GULLIES, GUTTERS and OVERFLOWS.

## BRICKWORK INDOORS

Brickwork indoors can be a highly attractive decorative feature, whether used for small areas like fire surrounds or for larger areas such as whole walls. If it is left natural, it can begin to look dirty, especially round fireplaces, and may benefit from being cleaned, repointed and resealed. If it has been painted over in the past, or has been exposed by the deliberate removal of existing plaster, it is virtually impossible to restore the brickwork to its natural state, so repainting is the only course of action open.

**ACTION**

**1** If the brickwork is natural and is to stay that way, scrub its surface thoroughly with a stiff bristle brush and household detergent. Rinse it down thoroughly. Do not use a wire brush as it will simply burnish the surface of the bricks.

**2** If the pointing is badly stained, rake it out carefully to a depth of about 6mm (¼in). If you do this evenly, you will expose clean mortar, which can be left on show: recessed pointing can look very dramatic. Otherwise, repoint it with ready-mixed bricklaying mortar or 1:6 (cement:soft sand) mixture.

**3** Seal the surface of the brickwork (after any repointing has dried) with polyurethane varnish or silicone water-repellent solution – the type usually used on exterior walls. Apply at least two coats. (This treatment is not suitable for fireplaces.)

**4** With painted or freshly-exposed brickwork, brush the surface down thoroughly. Then seal porous surfaces with a coat of masonry or stabilizing primer, followed by one or more coats of emulsion or masonry paint.

## BURSTS

Water pipes are most likely to burst in cold weather, when a plug of ice forms, expands and splits the pipe. The damage is not seen until the ice thaws and the leak begins. You are most likely to find a burst pipe on unlagged pipe runs in the loft, beneath ground-floor floorboards or against outside walls. Plumbing fittings on the pipe run may also be damaged.

**ACTION**

**1** Pinpoint the precise source of the leak.

**2** Find some way of containing the water while you work out which pipe run is affected.

**3** If it is on the rising main, turn off the stopcock – usually near the kitchen sink, or where the main enters the house.

**4** If it is on a pipe running from the storage cistern, turn off the stoptap on the outlet from the cistern; if there is no stoptap, tie up the ballvalve arm and empty the cistern by opening all the bathroom cold taps.

**5** When the leak stops, dry off the pipe and mark the split so you can find it again easily.

**6** Make a temporary repair by binding PVC tape round the pipe and adding a split piece of garden hose held on with wire.

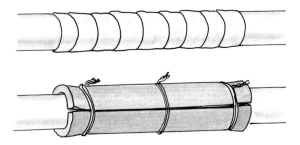

**7** Make a permanent repair by cutting out the split section of pipe and replacing it with a straight coupling (compression or capillary type) or with a new length of pipe between two straight couplings if the split is longer than about 12mm (½in). Alternatively, use a two-part epoxy pipe-repair resin.

**8** Restore the water supply and check that the leak has stopped.

**9** Make sure that the pipe is properly insulated so that it will not freeze again and cause further damage. Either wrap the pipe with bandage-type lagging or slip on lengths of foam pipe insulation.

Tape or tie bends and joins for complete protection.
See also FREEZE-UPS and PLUMBING.

## CABLE

It is important to understand the distinction between electric cable and flex (short for flexible cord). Electric cable links the various components of a domestic wiring installation, carrying current to socket outlets, lights and light switches. It may be buried in the plaster where it crosses walls, fixed beneath floorboards and above ceilings, or run on the surface (either unprotected or in slim plastic conduit). It has a tough oval PVC sheath (older cable has a rubber outer sheath, which crumbles with age) and the individual cores inside are also insulated. Two are colour-coded: one red, denoting the live core; the other black, denoting the neutral core. The third core – the earth continuity conductor – is bare, but is covered with slip-on sheathing colour-coded green and yellow when it is exposed at accessories. Flex is used to connect electrical appliances to the mains, normally via plugs at socket outlets, and to link light fittings to ceiling roses. Neither must ever be used to do the other's job. Cable comes in several sizes, each with a different current-carrying capacity and identified by the cross-sectional area of its copper conductors: $1mm^2$ cable is usually used for lighting circuits; $2.5mm^2$ cable for power circuits; larger sizes ($4mm^2$ and $6mm^2$) are for powerful appliances such as instantaneous showers and cookers. Although cable is tough, it can be damaged accidentally – most commonly by drilling through a hidden cable in a wall, or by driving a nail or screw through a cable underneath a floorboard. If this occurs, the circuit fuse will blow, and you may get a shock if you are using metal tools that make contact with the cable itself. Take care, therefore, to avoid cable runs if you can; you may find one vertically above or below any socket or switch, or crossing a floor joist in a notch just below the board surface.

**CABLE**

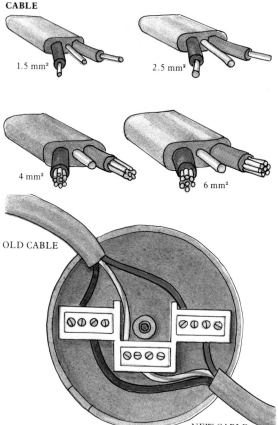

1.5 mm²

2.5 mm²

4 mm²

6 mm²

OLD CABLE

NEW CABLE

**ACTION**

1 If you hit an electric cable, the circuit fuse will blow and cut off the power to that particular circuit. Turn off the mains switch and remove the circuit fuse from the fuse box until you have repaired the damage.

2 If the cable is buried in plaster, trace the run up or down the wall, noting where it emerges into the floor or ceiling space and which accessory it supplies. Hack away some plaster if necessary; this will also

show if the cable is run in conduit or is simply plastered over.

**3** If the cable is run in conduit, you should be able to disconnect it from the accessory and then draw the cable up or down through the conduit. Tie a length of string to its end before pulling it out.

**4** Tie a length of new cable of the appropriate size to the string and draw the new cable through the conduit.

**5** In the floor or ceiling void, fit a three-terminal junction box to the side of a joist.

**6** Cut the old and new cables so they reach the box easily. Then strip the cores and connect them to the terminals: live cores to terminal 1, neutrals to terminal 2 and earths to terminal 3. Replace the box cover.

**7** If the cable is simply buried in the plaster, chop this away to reveal the whole cable run. Strip out the old cable, disconnecting it from the accessory and pulling it up or down into the floor or ceiling void as appropriate.

**8** Lay in new cable, protected by a length of cover strip, and repeat steps 5 and 6 to link the new cable to the existing cable. Plaster over the cable run.

**9** Reconnect the accessory to the new cable.

**10** If the damaged cable is under a floorboard, raise the board and fit a three-terminal junction box to the side of a joist next to the point of damage. Cut the cable, strip the cores and link them as in step 6.

**11** Replace the circuit fuse with fuse wire of the appropriate rating, put it back in its fuseholder and turn on the mains switch.

See also ELECTRICITY and FUSES.

## CARPET

Localized damage to carpets – for example, a cigarette burn – can often be repaired without recourse to professional help. The type of repair carried out will depend largely on the carpet's construction: it may be woven (Axminster or Wilton), tufted (tufts are secured into a fabric backing by a layer of latex foam or similar material) or bonded. Whatever the carpet type, you will need a small offcut in order to make the repair; if you have not kept any left-overs from when the carpet was laid, try to cut off a small piece from beneath an item of fitted furniture.

**ACTION**

**1** Find out whether the carpet is woven, bonded or tufted by lifting it in a corner of the room.

**2** If the damage is superficial, trim off the pile down to the backing.

**3** On long pile carpets, cut some tufts from the offcut, dip one end of the tufts in latex adhesive and position them in the hole left from step 2. Use a cocktail stick or similar implement to bed the tufts down firmly on the backing.

**4** When the adhesive has dried, trim the tufts to match the surrounding carpet.

**5** If the damage is more extensive, you will have to patch it. Lay your offcut over the damaged area, matching any pattern. Cut through offcut and backing using a sharp knife and straightedge.

**6** Lift the cut-out section from the carpet, and then work through the hole, sticking short lengths of carpet tape to the backing of the carpet.

**7** Coat the edges of the hole with latex adhesive to prevent fraying of the cut pile loops. Treat the edges of the patch in the same way.

**8** Lay the patch in place and hammer down all over to bond it securely to the carpet tape.

**9** Tease out the pile carefully along the edges of the patch so that it blends in with its surroundings.

## CASTORS

Many items of furniture are fitted with castors so they can be moved around easily. Two types are commonly in use: the peg type, where the castor locates in a socket in the frame of the furniture; and the plate type where it is screwed to the frame. With time or misuse, castors can jam or work loose.

**ACTION**

**1** Stiff castors may benefit from some lubrication. Do not use oil, though, since it will mark carpets and other floorings. Instead, use a spray-on aerosol lubricant, applied sparingly.

**2** With peg-type castors, the peg on the castor may drop out of its socket when the furniture is lifted. Prise out the socket and check the spring wire or nib at the upper end of the socket. You may be able to prise it out slightly so it will retain the castor peg.

**3** If the peg still drops out, you will have to replace castor and socket. This means replacing all the others on the piece as well, since single castors are rarely sold.

**4** If the wood surrounding the socket has split, force open the cracks and squeeze in woodworking adhesive. Cramp the repair and leave it to set before replacing the socket.

**5** With plate-type castors, the fixing screws may have come loose. Either glue thin dowel into the worn screw holes before refixing the castor or, if possible, refix it in a slightly different position to fresh wood.

**6** If castors mark carpet, sit them in castor cups or fit new castors with a greater load-bearing area.

## CERAMIC TILES

Ceramic tiles make an extremely durable wall or floor covering, but occasionally a tile may become loose or cracked as a result of accidental damage. In the former case, refixing the tile is quite straightforward. In the latter instance, you may have a spare tile kept from the original decoration, or else the tiles may still be on sale. Failing that, you will have to consider replacing the cracked tile with a contrasting new tile; if you replace several others at random, the whole effect will look quite deliberate.

**ACTION**

**1** If a tile is loose, lift it carefully. Soak it and then scrape off adhesive from its back and edges.

**2** Clean out the recess where the tile fitted, using a small cold chisel or scraper. Take care not to damage the tiles round the hole.

**3** Spread some ceramic tile adhesive in the recess.

**4** Press the tile down into the adhesive bed and tap it gently until it is level with its neighbours.

**5** Scrape away any excess adhesive and leave to set.

**6** After 24 hours, grout the gaps round the tile.

**7** If a tile is cracked, use a cold chisel to make a hole in its centre.

**8** Working carefully out towards the tile edges, chip away the cracked pieces of old tile. Take care not to damage surrounding tiles as you work.

**9** Remove old adhesive from the recess, spread fresh adhesive and bed the new tile in place as in steps 4, 5 and 6.

* See also GROUT.

## CHAIRS

In general, furniture repairs are best left to professional woodworkers and upholsterers unless the furniture is of a 'utility' nature. However, one of the commonest problems with everyday items concerns framed chairs and, in this case, simple and prompt repairs can restore the damage and make the chair perfectly serviceable again. The problem is open joints in the chair frame, caused by a combination of poor assembly and misuse – sitters leaning back on the rear legs in particular.

**ACTION**

**1** Where joints have begun to open up but no damage has yet been caused, knock the joints apart carefully with a hammer over a block of wood wrapped in fabric to protect the surfaces.

**2** Clean off all the tenons, and scrape the remains of old adhesive from the mortises.

**3** Brush PVA woodworking adhesive over the tenons, reassemble the joints and cramp them together while the adhesive sets. If you do not have any cramps, a simple tourniquet will do.

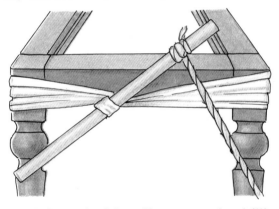

**4** Reinforce the joints if necessary by drilling through frame and tenon and inserting hardwood dowels, planed flush with the frame.

**5** If the frame or tenon has split, open up the cracks and inject woodworking adhesive. Then cramp the split section. Reassemble the joints as in step 3 when the repair has set.

**6** If the tenon is broken, cut away the broken remains. Then cut a slot in the end of the rail and insert a false tenon, dowelled into the rail for extra strength. Reassemble the joints as in step 3.

## CISTERNS

Cisterns store water in the loft for use throughout the house, and above WCs so they can be flushed at will. Modern water storage cisterns are made from plastic, which is not only corrosion-proof but is flexible enough to allow large cisterns to be passed through small loft openings when replacement is necessary. WC cisterns are nowadays made from ceramics or from plastic, and are likewise almost completely maintenance-free. However, old galvanized water storage cisterns can corrode and leak. Such a cistern should be replaced at the earliest opportunity, but when a leak occurs a makeshift repair allows the system to continue functioning and minimizes the damage a leak can cause.

**ACTION**

**1** As soon as the leak is noticed, pinpoint its source and mark the site of the leak on the cistern wall.

**2** Turn off the stopcock on the rising main feeding the cistern, or tie up the ballvalve arm if no stopcock is fitted.

**3** Open all bathroom cold taps to drain the cistern.

**4** If the leak is below the level of the lowest draw-off pipe, bale and mop out the remaining water.

**5** Wire-brush the tank surface inside and out in the area of the leak.

**6** Use a two-part epoxy resin repair kit to patch the leak, packing the material generously over the hole inside and outside the tank.

**7** Allow the repair to harden for the recommended time before refilling the cistern.

See also BALLVALVES, OVERFLOWS and PLUMBING.

## CONCRETE FLOORS

A properly laid solid concrete floor should incorporate a damp-proof membrane, and should provide a stable surface for whatever floorcovering is laid over it. However, if the damp-proof membrane is faulty or punctured, damp will begin to rise through it and will ruin floorcoverings in time. The surface may also begin to crack, or may become very dusty.

**ACTION**

**1** If the floor is damp, lift all floorcoverings and brush on a bitumen or pitch-epoxy damp-proofing liquid, following the manufacturer's instructions.

**2** Follow the membrane with a new mortar screed, or with a layer of floor-levelling compound (check first that it will be compatible with the damp-proofing membrane laid in step 1). Again, follow the manufacturer's instructions carefully.

**3** If cracks appear in the concrete floor surface, rake out loose material and undercut the edges of the crack so the mortar patch will adhere better. Brush PVA adhesive along the crack to improve the adhesion of the repair, then mix up a fairly dry mortar and trowel it into the crack. Smooth it off level with the floor surface and leave to harden.

**4** If a concrete floor surface is very dusty, seal it by brushing on one or two coats of proprietary concrete sealer after brushing away as much of the concrete dust as possible.

## CONDENSATION

Condensation is one of the biggest problems in many homes. Essentially, it occurs when warm moist air strikes a cool surface: the water vapour condenses on to the cold surface as water droplets. These not only cause dampness problems; they also ruin decorations, furnishings and clothes, encourage mould growth and adversely affect the health of the building's occupants. Ways of minimizing its effects include: eliminating cold surfaces on which condensation can form (such as large areas of ceramic tiles in bathrooms, or exposed water pipes); improving ventilation and increasing heating in affected rooms; and cutting down on the generation of moist air wherever possible.

# CONDENSATION

## ACTION

**1** Keep doors shut and windows open in steamy rooms.

**2** Vent clothes driers direct to the outside air.

**3** Use a ventilator hood over the cooker.

**4** Fit an extractor fan in the bathroom.

**5** Avoid flueless oil or paraffin heaters.

**6** Provide background heating in condensation-prone rooms.

**7** Line the inner surface of exterior walls with insulating board over a vapour barrier, to create warmer wall surfaces.

**8** Avoid putting wardrobes against outside walls, where condensation could form in or behind them.

**9** Install double glazing – ideally sealed units rather than secondary glazing.

**10** Have cavity wall insulation installed in cavity walls.

**11** Fit loft insulation, ensuring that the eaves are not blocked as condensation could occur in the loft, saturate the insulation and rot the timbers.

  See also CORK WALL TILES, DAMP and MOULD.

# CORK FLOORS

Cork tiles and strips provide a warm, resilient, splash-proof and attractive floorcovering that will last for years if properly laid. However, because of the nature of cork, it can be easily damaged by heavy impacts or by hot objects such as cigarettes. Localized damage can be repaired fairly easily.

## ACTION

**1** Remove localized stains, scars and marks by sanding the surface of the cork until the blemish has disappeared.

**2** Reseal the surface with three coats of polyurethane varnish or floor sealer, sanding down lightly between coats with fine glasspaper.

**3** If the damage extends over a larger area, lift the damaged tile or strip by cutting into it with a sharp knife and then prising it up with a flat-bladed scraper.

**4** Scrape up as much of the old adhesive as possible from the floor surface.

**5** Obtain a new tile that matches the existing ones as closely as possible, and test its fit; trim it to size if necessary.

**6** Spread contact adhesive (the emulsion type is safer than the solvent-based variety abused by glue-sniffers) on the back of the tile and the floor surface; leave until tacky.

**7** Press new tile into place flush with its neighbours.

**8** Seal the surface of the new tile with three coats of varnish or sealer, sanding lightly between coats.

## CORK WALL TILES

Cork tiles make an attractive wallcovering with the added bonus of providing a surface that is warm to the touch (and therefore less prone to condensation), absorbs sound to a certain extent and can be used as a pinboard or notice board if desired. Because the tiles are fixed with contact adhesive, they are very difficult to remove if a change of décor is wanted: the adhesive tends to pull the plaster away as well, and the result is often an unsightly mess that is expensive to put right. The best solution in this case is to cover the cork tiles with lining paper, which can then be painted or wallpapered over. If you are considering putting up cork tiles, you can avoid this problem in future by fixing the tiles to sheets of thin plywood or hardboard and then screwing these to the wall surface; it is then possible to unscrew the panels in the future (and to reuse them somewhere else).

**ACTION**

**1** If you must try to remove cork tiles, use a wide-bladed flat scraper held almost parallel to the wall surface to prise the tiles off. Do not use solvents to soften the old adhesive: they will not work, and can be a health and safety risk.

## CORK WALL TILES

**2** Remove stubborn lumps of old adhesive with a coarse abrasive disc fitted to a power sander; wear a mask as protection against the resultant dust. Fill hollows ready for redecoration.

**3** If you prefer to leave the tiles in place, brush size liberally on to the surface to seal it and reduce its porosity.

**4** Paste and hang heavy-duty lining paper over the tiles: vertically if you will be painting it, horizontally if you will be hanging another wallcovering over it.

● See also LINING PAPER.

## CORNICES

Ornamental cornices are an attractive feature of many older houses. Unfortunately, they are often clogged up with paint so that their detail is obscured, or else damaged locally, and replacements are extremely expensive. Restoring an original cornice can be a time-consuming job, but the end product is well worth all the effort.

**ACTION**

**1** If the cornice is clogged with old paint, test a small area with a wet sponge or spray it with a garden atomizer to see if the coating is washable distemper. If it is, soaking will soften the coating and it can be carefully picked away with an old screwdriver or clay modelling tool.

**2** If the cornice has been painted with modern emulsion or oil-based paints, use a thick paste paint stripper (the newest 'blanket' types are particularly effective) to clean up one length at a time. Follow the manufacturer's instructions at all times, and take steps to protect your hands with gloves and your eyes with goggles.

**3** Patch damaged areas with plaster of Paris, using a spatula or small filling knife to mould the plaster to match details elsewhere on the cornice. Tape polythene to the wall just below the cornice to protect existing wallcoverings while you strip and repair the cornice itself.

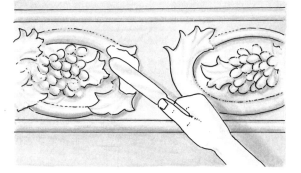

**4** Redecorate the cornice with emulsion paint, taking care not to apply it too thickly.
  ● See also MOULDINGS and STRIPPING PAINT.

## CRACKS IN WALLS AND CEILINGS

Small cracks in the plaster surface of walls and ceilings are common in almost every house. They are most commonly found at the join between walls and ceilings, radiating out from the corners of door and window openings and between walls and skirting boards. Cracks are caused by almost imperceptible movements in the house structure. In rare cases, the cause may be more sinister – the first signs of subsidence, for example – but this should only be suspected if the cracks are wider than about 3mm (⅛in) and are clearly getting bigger.

**ACTION**

**1** Use the edge of a small scraper to rake out loose material from the crack.

**2** Brush out any dust from the crack with a small paintbrush.

**3** Dampen the crack with clean water (plus some PVA adhesive).

**4** Mix up some interior filler or plaster to a fairly stiff consistency; if it is too wet it will slump from the crack.

## CRACKS IN WALLS AND CEILINGS

**5** Press it into the crack with a filling knife, leaving the filler slightly proud of the surface.

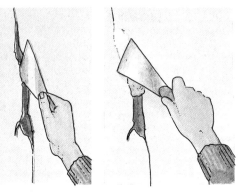

**6** When the filler has set, sand it down with fine glasspaper.

**7** For cracks at ceiling level, along skirting boards and round door and window frames, a flexible filler or mastic is the most effective. Rake out and prepare the crack as in steps 1-3, then pipe in the mastic and smooth it off with a damp finger.

**8** Cover persistent cracks at ceiling level by fitting a decorative cornice or coving.

## DAMP

Damp is an insidious enemy in the home. It can result from the presence of condensation, from moisture rising into the house from the ground beneath, or from water penetrating the supposedly weatherproof exterior of the house. Cures for damp are many and varied, but the problem has to be tackled in terms of long-term maintenance if it is to be eradicated completely. The action outlined below is intended only as a summary of the likeliest causes and their solutions.

### ACTION

**1** If solid ground floors are damp, suspect a failed damp-proof membrane in the floor.

**2** If ground-floor walls are damp up to waist height or thereabouts, with soggy decorations and mould growth in evidence, suspect a failed damp course in the walls. A chemical damp course can be quickly injected, but extensive internal replastering may be necessary. Underfloor timbers may be affected by wet or dry rot.

**3** If damp patches appear on walls after wet weather, suspect an external defect allowing water to penetrate. Depending on the location of the damp patch, the cause could be a defective chimney stack, porous or damaged flashings on roof slopes, cracked or missing roof tiles and slates, leaking or overflowing gutters, porous brickwork or rendering, gaps round door and window frames, or debris bridging the cavity of cavity walls. See under the appropriate heading for more details.

See also CONCRETE FLOORS, CONDENSATION and ROT.

## DECORATING

See under ANAGLYPTA, ARTEX, BRICKWORK, CARPET, CORK, CORNICES, CRACKS, DISTEMPER, FLOORCOVERINGS, HESSIAN, LAMINATES, LATH-&-PLASTER, LINCRUSTA, LINING PAPER, MIRRORS, MOULD, MOULDINGS, PAINTWORK, PLASTER, PLASTERBOARD, SKIRTINGS, STRIPPING PAINT, STRIPPING WALLCOVERINGS, VINYL FLOORS and WALLCOVERINGS.

## DISTEMPER

Distemper was the most widely used material for decorating walls and ceilings before the development of modern emulsion paints. Basically, there were two types of distemper: non-washable and washable. The former, often called whitewash

# DISTEMPER

though it could be coloured, is softened by water and so cannot be overpainted – or even papered over – successfully. The latter type was washable and therefore waterfast, and is less of a problem provided loose material is removed and the surface is sealed before redecoration.

**ACTION**

**1** If distemper is found, test it for type by rubbing with a damp cloth. Non-washable types will come off, others will not.

**2** Non-washable distemper must be removed. Scrub it thoroughly with water to soften it and work up a scum, which must then be wiped away. Rinse the surface thoroughly to remove all traces of the distemper. Then treat the surface with a multipurpose primer/sealer, followed by size if paperhanging.

**3** Washable distemper cannot be removed easily. Simply scrape off any loose material ready for redecoration.

# DOORS

Internal and external doors can suffer from a wide variety of faults, but two of the most common are binding and sticking, and warping. In the former case, the door literally jams when closed, sometimes along the edges, sometimes at a corner. In the latter case the door no longer fits snugly against the stop beads, with the result that it rattles and admits draughts. The cures are relatively simple.

**ACTION**

**1** If the door binds all the way round, the likeliest cause is a build-up of paint caused by successive redecoration without the previous coats of paint having been stripped first. The most satisfactory solution is to strip the whole door (quicker if it is removed from its hinges for treatment; quickest of all if it is sent away for dipping), but it is sometimes possible to plane just the leading edge: use an old plane, or a planer file, and take off about 3mm (⅛in) of wood as well as the paint to prevent future coats causing the same problem. Then prime, undercoat and repaint the door.

**2** If the door binds just at the top or bottom corners, the cause is probably moisture absorption through the unpainted top or bottom edge of the door; the problem is understandably worst in damp weather, least noticeable after a hot, dry spell. To cure it, take the door off its hinges and prime, undercoat and top-coat the edges thoroughly.

**3** If the door appears to have warped so that it does not sit snugly against the stop beads, do not attempt to correct the warp as it is not worth the effort. Instead, prise off the stop beads and pin them in place so they fit the door profile. On rebated frames this will not be possible; instead you will have to use draughtproofing to help correct the trouble.

  See also DRAUGHTPROOFING, HINGES and STRIPPING PAINT.

## DOWNPIPES

Downpipes carry rainwater from gutters at roof level down to gullies and soakaways on the ground. On older houses they are usually made of cast iron, but nowadays plastic is almost always used instead. At the top of a downpipe there is often a double bend (or offset) to take the pipe back against the wall from overhanging eaves. Then each length of pipe is supported by a bracket fixed to the wall; sections are a loose fit with each other. At the bottom end the pipe may discharge over an open gully via a shaped 'shoe', or may be piped directly into a trapped gully from where the water runs to underground drains or soakaways. Blockages can occur either at the top double bend or in the trap of a trapped gully, while damage to the downpipe may result in leaks partway down the run.

**ACTION**

**1** If water overflows from the gutter above the head of the downpipe, suspect a blocked offset. Climb a ladder to the eaves and carefully lift away the offset.

**2** Push out the blockage – usually leaves and wind-blown debris – and replace the offset after pushing a wire down the pipe to check that it is clear further down.

**3** If water is running out of the first downpipe join above ground level, suspect a blockage in the trapped gully (open-ended downpipes seldom get blocked at the shoe). Lift the gully grid and scoop out debris from the trap with a gloved hand. If the blockage does not clear, you will have to take down the last section of downpipe and clear it out with a wire or cane. Flush it through with water before replacing.

**4** If a length of downpipe is cracked as a result of accidental damage, you can patch it temporarily by wrapping waterproof repair tape or self-adhesive flashing tape round it. In the long-term, however, it should be replaced.

See also DRAINS, GUTTERS and LADDER SAFETY.

# DRAINS

The underground drains that take waste and soil water away from our homes seldom give trouble but, by the nature of the job they do, any problems can have rather unpleasant consequences. The first sign that anything is wrong is either an overflow from an inspection chamber (manhole) somewhere along the drain run, or from a yard gully that discharges into the drains. Once you have discovered the approximate site of the blockage it is a relatively simple matter to clear it.

**ACTION**

**1** If a gully is overflowing – and the trap is not blocked by debris – there is a blockage between it and the first manhole on the drain run. Check this by lifting the manhole cover; the chamber should be empty.

**2** Borrow or hire a set of drain rods. Attach a cane to the corkscrew head and feed it up the drain run from

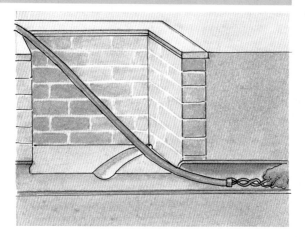

the manhole towards the gully, adding more rods as necessary. When the head reaches the blockage, rotate the rods clockwise (NEVER anti-clockwise, or they will unscrew and be lost in the drain) to break it up.

**3** Once water and debris flow down to the manhole, withdraw the rods and fit the brush head. Feed the canes back up the drain and scrub the run through, with water running into the gully from a garden hose to flush debris out.

**4** If a manhole is flooding, the blockage is further down the drain run. Check each manhole in turn until you find an empty one; the blockage is then between this one and the full one above it. Either rod the run out as in step 2, or fit a rubber plunger and rod it down from the full chamber. Scrub and flush the run through as in step 3 when the blockage is clear.

● See also BLOCKAGES.

# DRAUGHTPROOFING

A draughty house is a cold house, and with today's high fuel costs that means unnecessary waste of expensively warmed air. The biggest sources of draughts are ill-fitting windows and external doors, and draughtproofing round them will eliminate draughts very effectively. A word of warning is needed, however: in rooms containing fuel-burning appliances you must ensure that an adequate supply of air is provided so that the heater can burn efficiently. Over-zealous draughtproofing may starve the appliance of air and result in fumes that can be poisonous. Either fit an airbrick or ventilator near the appliance, or seek advice from your local fuel supplier or supply authority.

**ACTION**

**1** Draughtproof round windows with self-adhesive foam strip or other appropriate type; use bristle type excluders round sliding sash windows. Check that the window closes easily, and reposition catches if necessary.

**2** Draughtproof round external doors as for windows, adding a threshold excluder across the door bottom. Fit a brush-type excluder over the inside of letter box openings.

**3** Fit openable 'hit and miss' covers over airbricks, except in rooms with fuel-burning appliances; these can be closed in cold weather to cut draughts.

**4** If underfloor draughts are a problem, stick self-adhesive foam to one edge of quadrant beading. Pin the beading along the bottom of skirting boards so the foam compresses against the floor surface.

See also DOORS and MASONRY.

# DRAWERS

Drawers in old furniture often slide on the bottom edges of their sides and, if these edges become worn with use, the drawer will move unevenly and tend to stick. In more modern furniture side runners are usually fixed to the inside of the drawer recess; these engage in grooves cut in the drawer sides, and either the runners or the grooves may become worn, again resulting in uneven or stiff action of the drawer.

**ACTION**

**1** With bottom-sliding drawers, saw off the bottom edge of each drawer side with a tenon saw to leave a straight edge. Do not cut into the drawer front.

**2** Cut a new strip of wood thick enough to make up the original width of the drawer side. Glue and cramp it to the sawn edge of the drawer side. Leave to dry.

**3** When the adhesive has set, plane off the excess wood until the drawer slides smoothly. Then lubricate the bottom edge of the drawer with wax polish.

**4** If side runners are worn, unscrew them from the cabinet sides and cut new runners to match the groove width in the drawer sides. Plane them perfectly smooth and refix them inside the cabinet. Do not use adhesive; screws will hold them quite securely, and future replacement work will be easier. Lubricate the runners with wax polish.

## ELECTRICITY

When something electrical will not work in the home, tracking down the cause can be difficult if you are not fully aware of exactly how your wiring installation operates. This simple fault-finder will help your detective work and tell you what action is necessary in each case, and what precautions to take to avoid any danger until the fault is put right.

FAULT 1: pendant or other ceiling light will not work

**ACTION**

**1** Replace bulb.

**2** Check that the lighting circuit fuse is intact, or its circuit breaker is switched on. Replace fuse.

**3** Remove the circuit fuse or switch off the MCB (miniature circuit breaker), and then check the connections at the lampholder and ceiling rose. Remake connections if necessary.

**4** Check the flex continuity to see if there is a break (use a torch bulb and battery to check each core in turn). If necessary, replace the flex.

<u>FAULT 2:</u> plugged-in appliance will not work

**ACTION**

**1** Try the appliance at another socket.

**2** If it still does not work, replace the plug fuse.

**3** Check the flex connections within the plug, and remake them if necessary.

**4** Unplug the appliance and open up its casing to check the flex connections at the appliance terminal block. Remake them if they are loose or disconnected.

**5** Check the flex (as in step 4 under Fault 1).

**6** Check the power circuit fuse/MCB (as in step 2 under Fault 1).

**7** Isolate the appliance for repairs if the plug or circuit fuse blows again when the appliance is plugged in.

<u>FAULT 3:</u> a complete circuit is dead

**ACTION**

**1** Switch off all lights/disconnect all appliances on the circuit.

**2** Replace the circuit fuse or reset the MCB.

**3** Switch on the lights/plug in appliances again one by one, and note which one blows the circuit fuse or trips the MCB. Isolate the offending light or appliance, and check the points under Faults 1 and 2 as appropriate to repair it.

**4** With the circuit fuse out or the MCB off, unscrew the faceplates of accessories on the circuit to check for poor connections or signs of damage causing short circuits. Remake connections or replace damaged accessories as appropriate.

**5** If cable was damaged by drilling or nailing, replace affected cable.

**6** If all else fails, call in a qualified electrician.

<u>FAULT 4:</u> the whole installation is dead

**ACTION**

**1** Check to see if there is a local power cut.

**2** If you have an earth leakage circuit breaker fitted to the system, check to see if it has tripped off and reset it if it has. If it cannot be reset, this indicates a fault on the system. Check the action listed under faults 1, 2 and 3; if no fault is found, call electrician.

FAULT 5: an electric shock is received
**ACTION**
1 If the shock was from an appliance or accessory, isolate it until the fault is found and put right.
2 If the victim receives a severe shock, try to turn off the source of the power. If you cannot, then
3 grab the victim's clothing and pull him/her away from the power source. DO NOT touch his/her flesh with bare hands.
4 If the victim is conscious, keep him/her warm and call a doctor; DO NOT give food or drink.
5 If breathing or heartbeat has stopped, call an ambulance and give mouth-to-mouth resuscitation or thoracic compression until help arrives.
  See also CABLE, FLEX, FLUORESCENT LIGHTS, FUSES, LIGHTS, PLUGS, POWER POINTS and WIRING.

## EXPANDED POLYSTYRENE

Expanded polystyrene has been widely used in recent years as a decorative material, in the form of ceiling tiles, coving and ceiling and wall lining. For ceilings in particular, it offered a cheap and quick cover-up for poor surfaces, but is not as popular as it was and many people often want to replace it with other materials. It also acquired a bad reputation as a fire hazard; if improperly fixed and decorated it could cause flames – for example, from a chip pan fire – to spread extremely quickly across a ceiling and could help to propagate the fire as it burned. If such tiles and covings are to be installed, a fire-resistant grade should be chosen and a continuous bed of adhesive must be used, not occasional blobs. Finally, only emulsion paint (and ideally a fire-retardant grade) should be used to paint it; solvent-based paints should not be used.
**ACTION**
1 To take off old polystyrene tiles, coving or lining, use a scraper to remove as much of the material as possible.

## EXPANDED POLYSTYRENE

**2** Chip away hardened adhesive with a scraper, or sand it off with a coarse abrasive disc fitted to a disc sander attachment.

**3** Where removal damages the surface beneath, make good with filler or cover with wallcovering or textured finish.

• See also ANAGLYPTA, ARTEX, CRACKS and LINING PAPER.

## FIXINGS

Making firm fixings to walls and ceilings, doors and other surfaces round the house has never been easier, thanks to the wide range of fixing devices now available. To get good results, you have to be aware of the surface type involved so that you can choose the right fixing for the job. Here are some of the problems which you may encounter.

**ACTION**

**1** For medium or heavy-duty fixings to walls, drive screws into plastic wallplugs. Make sure that you use the correct drill size, and that you drill deep enough for the plug to penetrate solid masonry. Use a hammer drill to drill into concrete lintels or very hard masonry. Only use masonry nails if the fitting will be permanent.

**2** For medium and heavy-duty fixings to stud partition walls, either screw direct into the studs and noggings, or else fix a timber batten to the studs and then make subsidiary fixings to the batten.

**3** For light-duty fixings to stud partition walls, use spring or gravity toggles. Make sure the machine screw supplied is not too long for the thickness of the wall, and thread it through whatever you are fixing before inserting the toggle in the hole in the wall. Remember that the toggle will be lost in the cavity if the screw is withdrawn. However, some types have a collar which retains the toggle; this type is more appropriate if you want to take down the object fixed at a later date.

**4** For fixings to ceilings, either screw direct into

joists or into timber noggings fixed between joists.
5 For fixings into hollow doors, use small 'petal'
anchors that are threaded on to the screw, poked
into the fixing hole and drawn back against the inner
face of the door surface. Alternatively, use small
collapsible anchors. Make sure the screw is not too
long, or it will burst through the opposite face of the
door.

See also NAILS and SCREWS.

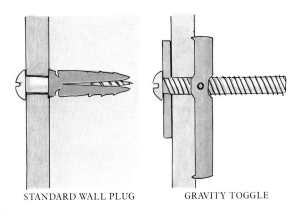

STANDARD WALL PLUG      GRAVITY TOGGLE

## FLEX

Flex (short for flexible cord) is used to connect
electrical appliances and pendant lights to the fixed
wiring. Flex can have two or three cores, all of which
are individually insulated within an outer sheath,
and it is important to choose the right type of flex
and the correct current rating for the job it has to do.
Two-core flex (with no earth core) is used with
double-insulated tools and equipment (things like
lawn mowers, hair driers and food mixers, all
marked with the □ symbol) and with non-metallic
pendant and table light fittings. All other appliances
are fitted with three-core flex. In most cases ordinary PVC-sheathed circular flex is used, but braided
and rubber-insulated flex is usually fitted to electric

39

heaters and fires, while unkinkable flex is normally used on kitchen appliances such as irons and kettles. Special heat-resistant flex is used for light fittings with high-wattage bulbs, and for connecting up immersion heaters. The table below gives the current-carrying capacity of each flex size, so you can choose the right type for the wattage of the appliance it is connected to, and also gives the maximum weight each size can support – vital information when you are hanging light fittings.

| Size (mm²) | Current (A) | Wattage | Max weight |
|---|---|---|---|
| 0.5 | 3 | up to 720 | 2kg (4½lb) |
| 0.75 | 6 | up to 1440 | 3kg (6½lb) |
| 1.0 | 10 | up to 2400 | 5kg (11lb) |
| 1.5 | 15 | up to 3600 | 5kg (11lb) |

**FLEX**

PARALLEL TWIN FLEX

TWO-CORE CIRCULAR FLEX

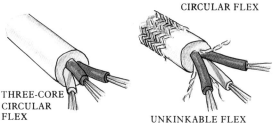

THREE-CORE CIRCULAR FLEX

UNKINKABLE FLEX

**ACTION**

**1** To replace worn or damaged flex, unplug the appliance or, for pendant lights, remove the lighting circuit fuse/switch off the circuit MCB.

**2** Purchase the required length of the appropriate type of flex.

**3** Strip back the flex sheath carefully to the required distance. Tape braided sheaths.

**4** Strip the core insulation carefully, taking care not to cut the cores. Twist the strands neatly together.

5 Connect the flex cores to the appliance terminals (brown to the live terminal, usually marked L; blue to the neutral terminal, marked N; green/yellow to the earth terminal, marked E or ⏚). Remember to thread it through the cord grip, fitted to protect the flex where it enters the appliance casing.

6 Connect the other end of the flex to the plug.

7 If you have to extend a flex, use a proper flex connector. Do not simply link the cores and tape the join. Use a one-part connector for a permanent join, a two-part one if you will want to disconnect the extension. With two-part extensions, make sure the part with the pins is linked to the appliance and the part with the sockets is connected to the plug end of the flex.

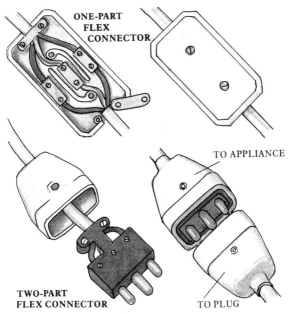

ONE-PART
FLEX
CONNECTOR

TO APPLIANCE

TWO-PART
FLEX CONNECTOR

TO PLUG

8 If flex is damaged, do not tape the damage up; cut it out and link the two cut ends with a one-piece connector, or else replace the flex completely.

See also ELECTRICITY, PLUGS and LIGHTS.

## FLOORS

Most houses have suspended timber floors, consisting of boards nailed to timber joists spanning each room. Some ground floors are solid, especially in modern houses, and in blocks of flats all floors may be concrete. Concrete floors seldom give much trouble, but timber floors may need occasional attention if they creak, are uneven or have gaps between the boards.

**ACTION**

**1** If boards bang or creak, the fixing nails have probably worn loose, allowing the board to move slightly when walked on. Drive loose nails home with a nail punch and hammer. Take care if driving in extra nails not to pierce hidden cables or pipes: it is best to lift the loose board completely to look for these before refixing it to its joists. Use screws rather than nails to hold boards that have warped slightly.

**2** If the floor surface is uneven and board lines are showing through floorcoverings, lift the floor-covering and cover the boards with sheets of hardboard held in place with hardboard nails. Condition the sheets first by brushing water on to the mesh side and leaving the sheets stacked back to back overnight. Then lay them mesh side down with staggered joints, pinning them at intervals all round the edges and across the sheets.

**3** If the floor surface is to be exposed as a decorative feature, remove dirt and stains by using a floor sander – a machine resembling a lawnmower, which can be hired.

**4** If gaps have opened up between the boards, either fill the gaps with thin strips of wood glued and tapped into place and planed down flush with the floor surface, or lift and re-lay the boards tightly together. In the latter case you will need a new board to fill the gap left at one side of the room when the old boards have been re-laid.

See also CONCRETE FLOORS and STAIRCASES.

## FLOORCOVERINGS

See under CARPET, CERAMIC TILES, CORK FLOORS, VINYL FLOORS and WOODBLOCK FLOORS.

## FLUORESCENT LIGHTS

Fluorescent lights offer two main advantages over tungsten lamps: even, shadow-free lighting and low running cost. They emit more light per watt of power consumed than tungsten lamps, and the tubes have a comparatively long life. When they do malfunction, the problem is usually simple to solve.

**ACTION**

**1** If the tube flickers, is reluctant to light or glows at each end but fails to light fully, fit a new starter. This is a small cylinder that is located in the side of the fitting, and is removed by turning it anti-clockwise. Take it to the shop so you can buy an identical type.

**2** If the tube shows signs of blackening at the ends, it is probably nearing the end of its useful life. Replace it with a new tube of the same length, colour and wattage.

**3** If the tube glows at one end, check the tube connections. If the pin holders are damaged or bent, fit a new holder.

**4** If the fitting is emitting a hot oily smell, the choke may be burning out. This is a rectangular component within the base of the fitting, and is usually simple to disconnect and replace. As with the starter, make sure you fit an identical replacement.

See also ELECTRICITY.

## FREEZE-UPS

The first sign of a frozen pipe is when water will not flow from a tap on the affected pipe run. Finding the precise point at which the pipe has frozen can be difficult (although if the ice has burst it, you will soon find the point when it starts to leak once thawing begins). The best method is to work back along the pipe run from the affected tap, leaving it open so that water will start to flow if and when you reach the ice plug. Before you start looking for the plug make sure you know what to do if the pipe has burst.

**ACTION**

**1** Starting at the affected tap, play a fan heater or powerful hair drier on to a short section of the pipe.

**2** Feel the pipe as you proceed, looking out for any signs of splits or slight swellings. Mark any you find so you can locate them easily if repairs are necessary.

**3** If water starts to drip from the tap, you are near the site of the freeze-up. Play the warm air back and forth over the pipe until water is flowing freely.

**4** Insulate the pipe immediately to prevent another freeze-up if temperatures are very low. If you cannot purchase pipe bandage or sleeving, try to wrap it with rags, sacking or other material, or leave a heater on in the vicinity – if this can be done safely.

See also BURSTS, LEAKS and PLUMBING.

# FUSES

Each electrical circuit in the home is protected against overloading and other electrical faults by a circuit fuse or, in the most modern installations, by a miniature circuit breaker (MCB). The fuse is a length of special wire that melts if a fault causes it to overheat, and so cuts off the current to the circuit concerned. An MCB is an electrical switch that trips to 'off' in the event of a fault, again cutting off the current. Each circuit has a fuse of a different rating – 5A (amps) for lighting circuits, 15A or 20A for radial circuits to appliances such as immersion heaters, 30A for ring and radial circuits to socket outlets and 45A to large cookers. In addition to the circuit fuses, most homes have socket outlets that accept plugs with rectangular pins, and these contain a small fuse that will blow in the event of a fault on the appliance.

Two common ratings exist for these tiny cartridge fuses: 3A for appliances rated at less than 750W (watts), and 13A for other more powerful appliances. It is vital to be prepared for the occasion when a fuse blows. So, next to the fusebox, keep the following: a small torch, an electrical screwdriver, fuse wire of the appropriate rating for all your circuits (or a supply of cartridge circuit fuses if your system uses them), plus a number of plug fuses of each size.

**ACTION**

**1** To repair a circuit fuse, switch off the mains switch and pull out each fuseholder in turn. When you find the blown fuse, remove the remains of the old fuse wire and clean out any charred bits.

**2** Feed in a length of new fuse wire of the correct rating and wind each end round the terminal before tightening up the screw. Do not pull the wire taut.

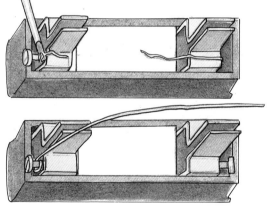

**3** Trim off the unwanted ends neatly, then replace the fuse holder in the fuse box and restore the power.

**4** With MCBs, simply reset tripped switch to 'on'.

**5** With cartridge fuses you may not be able to see at a glance which fuse has blown. You can test a suspect fuse by holding it across the open end of a switched-on metal-cased torch with one metal cap on the casing and the other on the end of the battery. A sound fuse will light the torch; a blown one will not.

**6** When you have found the blown fuse, replace it by pressing in a new fuse of the correct rating and put back the fuse holder.

**7** If the fuse blows or the MCB trips off again as soon as the power is restored, the fault is still present. NEVER use any other metallic material to repair a blown fuse. You may succeed in restoring power at the time: in the future your stupidity may kill you or a member of your family because the fuse will not blow when it should in the event of a fault.

See also ELECTRICITY and PLUGS.

## GAS SAFETY

Gas enters the house through a service pipe, where it is connected to your gas meter. From the meter the gas is piped through iron or copper pipes to wherever it is needed in the house. The only part of the installation you are allowed to touch is the main control cock next to the meter; this cuts off the gas supply to the house, and it is vital that you know where it is so you can turn off the supply if you suspect a leak. You may also find small 'butterfly' valves on the gas pipes to individual appliances.

**ACTION**

**1** If you suspect a gas leak, put out cigarettes, matches and naked flames (including cooker and boiler pilot lights).

**2** Open doors and windows to disperse the gas.

**3** Check to see if an appliance tap has been left on.

**4** If not, suspect a leak from the pipework, and turn off the gas supply at the main control cock. In most cases this means moving the handle from its 'on' position in line with the pipework to the 'off' position at 90° to the pipe (in some cases you have to move the handle through 180°).

**5** Call your local gas emergency service, but do not use your own phone – this could cause an explosion. Until the engineers come, leave windows open and do not strike any naked flame or operate any electrical equipment – a slight spark could cause an explosion.

## GLASS

When a pane of glass is broken or cracked, it should be replaced at the earliest opportunity. A broken pane could cause an injury (and will let wind and rain in), while a cracked pane could shatter unexpectedly, showering sharp fragments on an unsuspecting passer-by. When you order replacement glass, make sure you order the right thickness. As a guide use 3mm thick glass for panes measuring up to about $1m^2$ ($10\frac{3}{4}$ sq ft) in area; 4mm glass for panes up to $2.6m^2$ (28 sq ft) provided that the maximum length of one side does not exceed 2.1m (7ft); 6mm glass for panes over $2.6m^2$ in area. Give measurements for the pane in metric units, not feet and inches; metric measurements are more accurate and less prone to misinterpretation. If you are buying patterned glass, make sure you specify which way the pattern runs.

**ACTION**

**1** When a pane is broken, pick up all the pieces and wear stout gloves to pull out jagged remnants from the frame. Wrap them in newspaper and place them in the dustbin.

**2** If replacement glass cannot be ordered at the time, cover the opening with hardboard, plywood or polythene according to its size and location.

**3** Clean out the rebate in the frame with an old chisel or a glazier's hacking knife, removing all the old putty and pulling out any glazing sprigs that were holding the glass in place. Prime any bare wood you expose.

**4** Measure each edge of the rebate accurately, write down the figures and use the smaller one if they differ to specify the glass size. Deduct 3mm from each measurement to allow for a slight clearance gap all round.

**5** Order the glass, plus about 450g (1lb) of putty for

each metre of rebate length. Buy linseed oil putty for wood windows, metal casement or all-purpose putty for metal ones.

**6** Squeeze some putty into the rebate all round the opening.

**7** Press the new pane into place by pressing the edges, not the centre of the pane, and tap in a glazing sprig or fit a spring clip (metal windows only) every 300mm (12in).

**8** Press in more putty all round the rebate and smooth it off neatly at an angle of about 45° with a putty knife.

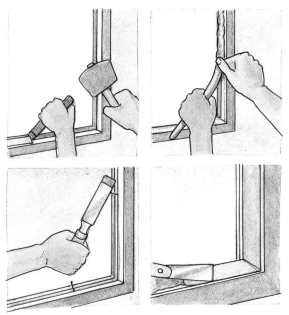

**9** Mitre the corners neatly, trim off excess putty on the inside of the window and brush over the putty surface with a moistened paint brush to seal the putty to the glass.

**10** After two or three weeks, prime, undercoat and paint over the new putty.

See also LEADED LIGHTS and PUTTY.

## GROUT

Grout is used to fill the narrow gaps between ceramic wall and floor tiles once they have been bedded in place. Some tile adhesives can also be used as grout, otherwise a separate product is required. Grout may crack and fall out, or may become stained and discoloured. Special quality grout is used on ceramic tile worktops where food is being prepared.

**ACTION**

**1** If grout is cracked or missing, rake along the grout lines with an old screwdriver or similar implement to dislodge any loose grout.

**2** Brush out debris with a soft brush.

**3** Use a plastic spreader to force new grout into the gaps between the tiles, scraping the grout across each grout line and removing excess as you work. Smooth it off with a dowel.

**4** Leave the grout to harden, then polish off excess with a clean dry cloth.

**5** If grout is stained, brush on a dilute solution of household bleach, leave to work and then rinse off. If this does not work, you can either experiment by brushing on emulsion paint to restore the grout's colour (wipe excess off the tiles as you work) or rake out the stained grouting and re-grout. If staining occurs quickly, you could experiment with coloured grout which would not show up stains so quickly.

See also CERAMIC TILES.

## GULLIES

Gullies, into which waste pipes and downpipes discharge, are usually covered with a metal or plastic grating intended to stop debris being blown into the gully and blocking the trap below ground level (this, like an appliance trap, stays full of water to keep drain smells out). However, debris tends to accumulate in the trap, and can lead to a blockage. If this occurs, the gully will overflow. If the pipes discharge over the grating, an overflow will also occur if the grating becomes covered with leaves.

**ACTION**

**1** If the gully overflows, lift the grating and reach down into the gully with a gloved hand to scoop out debris from the bottom of the trap.

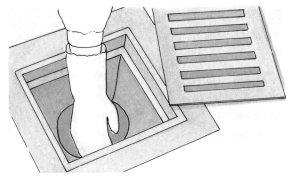

**2** When you have cleared the blockage, scrub the sides of the gully out with washing soda to remove grease and scum.

**3** Flush the gully through with clean water, scrub the grating and replace it.

**4** If the pipes discharge over the grating, extend them so they discharge below it; you will have to cut holes in the grid to allow them to pass through. Then make up a plywood or plastic cover to fit over the gully surround and help keep debris out in future.

See also BLOCKAGES and DRAINS.

## GUTTERS

Gutters can become blocked with debris washed off the roof surface or blown in by the wind, and by moss – growing unseen from ground level. They may also be damaged by carelessly placed ladders, may overflow if the brackets sag and may leak at joints. To work on them safely, use a ladder fitted with a stay that holds the top of the ladder away from the wall.

**ACTION**

**1** Climb carefully to eaves level and scoop out debris from the gutter with a garden trowel or gloved hand. Empty the debris into a bucket hanging from the ladder.

**2** Start at the highest point of the gutter run and hose the gutter down with water from a garden hose, using a scrubbing brush if necessary to leave the inside of the gutter clean.

**3** If the gutter is cracked, effect a temporary repair with self-adhesive flashing tape (dry the gutter surface first). Aim to replace the damaged length in due course.

**4** If joints leak, remake them (plastic systems), checking that the rubber sealing strip is in place, or seal the joint (metal systems) with bituminous mastic.

**5** If the gutter is sagging at any point because the brackets are loose or missing, refix the bracket if possible or fit a repair bracket, screwed on to the fascia board, to restore the correct gutter slope. In an emergency, drive a stout screw into the fascia immediately below the gutter to hold it up.

● See also DOWNPIPES and LADDER SAFETY.

## HESSIAN

Hessian is a popular coarsely woven fabric wall-covering, usually paper-backed and available in a natural oatmeal colour and in a range of dyed shades. It is very hardwearing, needing only to be brushed or vacuum-cleaned occasionally to keep it clean and in good condition. However, when it is time for a change of décor, you may want to re-decorate or remove it entirely.

**ACTION**

**1** Hessian can be overpainted with emulsion or solvent-based paints and this is the simplest way of redecorating it. Use a long-pile roller – it will force paint into the weave more efficiently than a brush.

## HESSIAN

**2** Hessian can be stripped from the wall by lifting a corner or seam and carefully pulling off complete lengths. If the paper-backed variety was hung, soak and scrape the backing as for ordinary wallcoverings. If the hessian has been painted, it should still strip in complete sections, but in stubborn cases a steam stripper will speed results.

See also ANAGLYPTA.

## HINGES

Hinges that are incorrectly fitted can make a door difficult to shut, or can cause the door to swing instead of standing in one position. Squeaky hinges do not cause such trouble, but can be extremely annoying if not attended to.

**ACTION**

**1** If a door is difficult to shut smoothly, check first that the heads of the screws securing the hinges are driven straight and fully home. If they protrude, they will prevent the two hinges from meeting. Drive in any loose screws, drilling fresh pilot holes if they are crooked.

**2** If the door's hinged edge meets the frame before the door is fully closed, the hinge recesses are too deep. Remove the hinges, pack the recesses out with cardboard or hardboard, and replace the hinges.

**3** If the hinge leaves meet before the door is fully closed, the hinge recesses are too shallow. Remove the hinges, chisel out the recesses slightly and replace the hinges.

**4** If the door swings open or shut unaided, the hinges are not vertically above one another. Remove one hinge, pack the old screw holes with lengths of glued dowel and reposition the hinge slightly further in or out so as to align it with the other one.

**5** If the door squeaks, spray each hinge with aerosol lubricant (do not use oil, which can drip and mark paintwork and floor-coverings). Replace badly worn hinges with new ones the same size.

See also DOORS.

## JOINTS IN PLUMBING

On modern copper plumbing systems, joints are made either with soldered capillary fittings or with compression fittings. The former are made of copper, are little wider than the pipe they join and are formed by heating the fitting (which contains a ring of solder inside each end) with a blowlamp. The latter are made of brass, are much more obtrusive (and more expensive) and are assembled by tightening a cap nut on to the fitting; this crushes a small metal ring called an olive down on to the pipe and makes the joint watertight. Either type may begin to leak if frozen or wrenched.

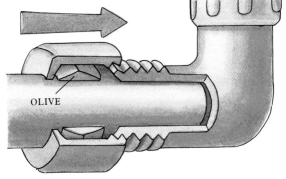

OLIVE

**ACTION**

**1** If a capillary joint leaks, drain the affected pipe of water.

**2** Dry the pipe and fitting thoroughly.

**3** Heat the leaking end of the fitting with your blowlamp, and feed cored solder wire into the gap between fitting and pipe. Do this quickly, since you do not want the other end of the fitting to overheat and melt its soldered seal.

**4** If this fails, it is best to remake the connection with a new capillary fitting with integral solder ring. Heat up the old fitting until the solder runs out; then spring it out of the pipe ends (wear gloves as it will be hot) and insert the new fitting after cleaning up the pipe ends and applying flux to them. Heat the fitting with the blowlamp until a ring of solder appears round each join. Leave to cool, then restore the water supply.

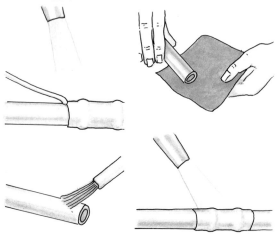

**5** With compression fittings, try tightening the cap nut slightly with a spanner.
**6** If this fails, drain the pipe and undo the cap nut. Slide it back to expose the olive, and cut this off carefully with a hacksaw.

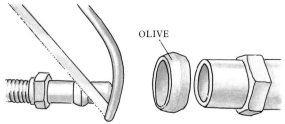

OLIVE

**7** Spring the pipe out of the fitting, slip on a new olive and insert the pipe in the fitting again.
**8** Slide the olive up against the fitting. Then wrap some PTFE plumber's tape round the thread of the fitting (not essential, but an extra help in getting a waterproof joint) and hand-tighten the cap nut.

**9** Grip the fitting with one wrench, and tighten the cap nut by 1¾ turns with another wrench. Restore the water supply. Tighten further if necessary.

● See also BURSTS, PLUMBING and RADIATORS.

## LADDER SAFETY

Whenever you are using a ladder, make sure that it is in good condition (especially timber ladders) and that you set it up and secure it properly before you climb it. More accidents in and around the home are caused by falls from ladders than any other activity. Do not climb ladders at all if you suffer from vertigo.

**ACTION**

**1** Carry the ladder to where it is wanted, and set it against the wall.

**2** Make sure that the bottom is on level ground so that the ladder will stand vertically. On hard ground, stand it on sacking; on soft ground, use a board with a batten nailed across to stop the ladder feet sinking in.

**3** Position the foot of the ladder 1m (1yd) out from the base of the wall for every 4m (4yd) of ladder height.

**4** Rope the top of the ladder to a window frame or to a stout screw eye driven into the fascia. Do not trust a downpipe.

**5** When you climb the ladder, keep your arms straight so that your body is roughly vertical. Carry tools etc. in pockets or in an apron; do not carry them in your hands.

**6** Use a ladder hook to suspend paint cans so that you have one hand to hold the ladder as you work.

**7** Do not lean out too far; keep your hips within the line of the ladder stiles.

**8** Store a ladder horizontally, either flat (supported by garage roof members, for example) or on edge on wall brackets beneath the lower stile. Do not suspend it by its upper stile, or the rungs may become loose.

## LAMINATES

Plastic laminates make extremely hard-wearing and attractive worktops, but they can be damaged by heat: for example, hot pans, irons and cigarettes. Provided they are well stuck down, it is easier to cover damaged laminate with a new sheet, rather than remove it.

**ACTION**

**1** If the damage is slight, you may be able to remove it by using a scouring pad and some abrasive cleaner.

**2** For more major damage, try to obtain some matching laminate (or at least a similar pattern – easiest with woodgrains and plain colours). You may be able to order a cut-to-size piece, but you are more likely to have to buy at least half a full-size sheet.

**3** Cut the new laminate roughly to size, allowing an extra 3mm (⅛in) or so in each dimension.

**4** Thoroughly clean and degrease the existing laminate surface, and rub it all over with wet-and-dry paper to provide a key for the adhesive.

**5** Spread contact adhesive over both the old worktop and the back of the new laminate. Leave it to become tacky.

**6** Position one edge of the new laminate on the worktop, and then lower the sheet into place carefully. Press it down thoroughly all over.

**7** Trim the edge of the laminate with a sharp plane or a laminate trimmer; leave a neat 45° bevel.

## LATH-AND-PLASTER

Lath-and-plaster walls and ceilings are made by pinning slim laths between ceiling joists or wall studs, and then forcing plaster on to the laths; as the surface is smoothed over, some of the plaster squeezes through between the laths to form a key that holds the plaster layer in place. Accidental damage can break the laths, leaving a hole. Use plasterboard to replace damaged areas.

**ACTION**

**1** Using a padsaw, cut a rectangular hole round the damage, as far as the joist or studs at each side.

**2** Nail lengths of 50mm (2in) sq timber between the joists/studs at each end of the hole, and to the joists/studs at each side.

**3** Cut a patch of plasterboard to fit the hole, and nail it in place with plasterboard nails.

**4** Tape the joints and cover the patch with plaster.

## LEADED LIGHTS

Leaded light windows consist of small panes of glass held in a lattice of grooved lead called 'cames'. Individual panes can be broken, while cleaning can, over the years, cause the whole pane to bulge.

**ACTION**

**1** To remove a broken pane, cut through the cames diagonally at each corner with a sharp knife, and use an old chisel to open the cames.

**2** Lift out the pieces of broken glass and brush out the remains of the old bedding putty.

**3** Establish the size of the new pane by measuring to the centre of the came at each side and subtracting 3mm from each measurement. On irregular-shaped windows, make a paper or cardboard template and take that to your glass merchant.

**4** Slot the new piece of glass into the unopened came at the top, press into place against the others and gently bend the opened cames back into place. Trim off the surplus bedding putty.

**5** Burnish the cut corners with steel wool or emery paper, apply flux and use a soldering iron to run a little solder into each joint. Finish off the corners neatly by gently rubbing over the intersection of the cames with the tip of the soldering iron.

**6** If a leaded light pane has become bowed, cut two pieces of plywood to match the size of the pane. Get a helper to hold one against the pane on the inside, while you press the other against the outside to force the cames back to a true vertical.

## LEAKS

Leaks in your plumbing or heating system can occur at a wide variety of sites: on pipework, at fittings, taps, radiators, cisterns and so on. Your first action when a leak occurs should be to minimize the damage by containing the water if possible, by lifting floorcoverings and moving furniture in danger, and by draining the pipework supplying the leak to stop the flow of water. What you do next depends on the site of the leak.

● See also BALLVALVES, BURSTS, CISTERNS, DOWNPIPES, FREEZE-UPS, GUTTERS, JOINTS, OVERFLOWS, PIPES, RADIATORS, SHOWERS, TAPS and WASHERS.

## LIGHTS

In most houses, two lighting circuits are provided: one for the ground floor rooms, one for upstairs rooms. Each should supply a maximum of eight lighting points. Wall lights may be wired as extensions of the lighting or the power circuits; make sure you know which light is on which circuit, so you know what action to take if one should fail.

● See also ELECTRICITY and FLUORESCENT LIGHTS.

## LINCRUSTA

Lincrusta is a relief wallcovering manufactured from a mixture of fillers and linseed oil which is pressed into sheets with the design on one surface and allowed to harden. It comes in stiff rolls, and is fixed to the wall with special adhesive. It is usually painted over and, like many other relief wall-coverings, is quickly redecorated with another coat of paint. However, for a complete change of décor it must be removed completely.

**ACTION**

**1** Use a steam wallpaper stripper to soften the Lincrusta.

**2** As each area is treated, use a broad-bladed flat scraper to remove as much material as possible.

**3** Treat stubborn areas again with the steam stripper; the paper backing should begin to lift too.

**4** As you will find it difficult to remove all traces of the adhesive, be prepared to line the walls before redecorating.

● See also LINING PAPER.

## LINING PAPER

Lining paper is used to provide a perfect surface for hanging certain types of wallcovering, and also as a way of preparing less-than-perfect wall surfaces for subsequent redecoration. White lining paper comes in light, medium and heavy grades (often referred to by grade as 360, 480 and 600) and in two finishes, one of which is called extra white and is suitable for taking emulsion paint. Coloured linings are also available. Reinforced lining paper is bonded to a fine cotton or linen scrim, and is used to line walls subject to excessive cracking or movement. When another wallcovering is to be hung over the lining, the lining is hung horizontally so that the joins will not show through. Successive lengths are butt jointed. Lining paper is hung with the same paste as the final wallcovering.

**ACTION**

**1** Wash down the surface to be lined with detergent, and rinse off with clean water. Allow to dry.

**2** Treat surface with a coat of size (use paste diluted to the correct consistency if recommended by the paste manufacturer).

**3** Cut first strip of lining paper to match wall width, paste and fold into concertinas.

**4** Set up trestles spanning the width of the wall.

**5** If right-handed, start at the top right-hand corner and brush the end of the length into place.

**6** Work across the wall, brushing the paper into place as you go from the centre of the length towards the top and bottom edges. If the ceiling line is uneven, keep the top edge of the lining paper just below the ceiling line.

**7** Trim the end of the paper with scissors when you reach the opposite corner. Brush flap into place.

**8** Hang successive lengths in the same way, finishing off with the last strip trimmed to reach to just above the skirting board. Allow to dry out thoroughly before hanging the final wallcovering.

See also CORK WALL TILES.

## LOCKS

Most front doors have a cylinder nightlatch, mounted on the inside face of the door, and a mortise lock which is set into the door edge. For the security of your home – and for your peace of mind – it is vital that these locks should work efficiently. Regular maintenance should ensure smooth operation, but sometimes a lock will stick and may ultimately need replacing.

**ACTION**

**1** Every six months, lubricate locks with powdered graphite. Put some graphite on the key, insert it and turn several times.

**2** If a lock sticks, test it with the door open. If it works properly, check that the bolt and striking plate (or staple for a rim lock) are correctly aligned.

**3** If they are out of alignment, unscrew the striking plate/staple. Reposition as necessary, chiselling out extra wood from the frame as required.

**4** If a mortise lock still sticks – or if there was no alignment problem – unscrew the face plate from the edge of the door and remove.

**5** Undo the lock-retaining screws beneath the plate and gently prise out the lock with a screwdriver.

**6** Release the screws in the lock side plate and lift off.

**7** Check the mechanism for worn parts, broken spring, dirt and grit.

**8** If nothing is obviously wrong, clean the lock, reassemble it and test it with the key.

**9** If the lock still refuses to function, have it repaired or replace it.

**10** If you buy a new one, obtain the identical make and model so that it fits into the same recess. To refit, follow steps 4 and 5 in reverse.

**11** To remove a cylinder rim lock, unscrew the lock case either from the inside or the edge of the door.

**12** Release the connecting screws and push out the cylinder. Undo and remove the mounting plate.

## MASONRY

Where door and window frames meet solid masonry, it is always difficult to seal the gap so as to prevent moisture and draughts from getting in. This is because the two materials – wood and masonry – tend to expand and contract at different rates as temperature and humidity alter, and so any rigid filler simply cracks and falls out. The solution is to use a flexible non-setting mastic that will accommodate the movement and adhere to both surfaces.

**ACTION**

**1** Rake out the gap between frame and wall to remove loose material.

**2** If the gap is deep, pack it out with mortar to within 6mm (¼in) of the surface and allow to harden.

**3** Pipe non-setting builder's mastic from a cartridge gun into the gap, making sure that it is completely filled and that the mastic sticks to both surfaces. Smooth it over if necessary with a piece of dowel dipped in water.

See also BRICKWORK and FIXINGS.

## METAL

If you want to paint metalwork inside or outside the house, you must prepare the surface properly otherwise the paint will just flake off again. This preparation will involve the removal of rust or other surface damage, followed by the correct primer. The check-list below will help you choose the right primer for the type of metalwork being treated.

| Surface | Primer |
| --- | --- |
| New iron and steel | calcium plumbate primer (outdoors) zinc chromate primer (indoors) |
| Bitumen-coated metal | aluminium spirit-based sealer |
| Galvanized iron | calcium plumbate primer |
| Aluminium | zinc chromate or zinc phosphate primer |
| Copper and brass | no priming needed |
| Lead | allow to weather; no priming needed |

**ACTION**
1 Degrease metal surface with white spirit.
2 Remove rust by brushing on chemical rust remover, or by using wire brush attachment in electric drill.
3 Apply primer, following instructions on tin.
4 Apply undercoat and top coat.
  See also RUST and WROUGHT IRON.

## MIRRORS

When hanging mirrors or mirror tiles, two completely different approaches need to be taken. With mirrors, it is important that any fixings are strong enough to support the weight of the mirror, yet are not so tight that they might crack it. With mirror tiles the problem lies in ensuring that the tiles are perfectly level, otherwise the reflection will be seriously distorted.

**ACTION**
1 If you are hanging a mirror with mirror screws, mark the positions for the screw holes carefully.

Then drill them precisely: if they are off line the screws may crack the mirror as they are driven in.

**2** If the wall surface is at all uneven, the mirror will crack if the screws are tightened fully. Avoid this either by fitting a tap washer behind each screw, or by sticking strips of self-adhesive foam draught strip to the back of the mirror. Both will take up any unevenness in the wall surface, and will also allow air to circulate behind the mirror and help stop condensation forming.

**3** Drive the screws until the mirror is securely held. Then add the domed covers.

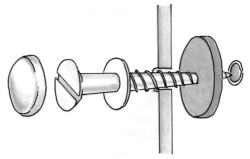

**4** You will get better results when hanging mirror tiles if you mount them on a plywood backing board rather than directly on the wall. When all the tiles are in place and you are satisfied that the reflection is not distorted, mount the complete panel by screwing it to battens fixed to the wall. If you want the fixing screws to be concealed, leave the border tiles off until you have mounted the panel and then fix them in place to cover the screw heads.

See also FIXINGS and SCREWS.

## MOULD

Mould growth occurs on surfaces round the house that are prone to condensation: cold but badly ventilated areas behind cupboards and wardrobes, for example, and on window frames. The wind-blown

# MOULD

spores need only moisture to survive. Preventing their growth is largely a matter of avoiding the conditions in which they flourish but, if they do start to spread, killing the spores can at least deter them.

**ACTION**

**1** Wash or scrub down affected surfaces with a dilute solution of household bleach, leaving the liquid on the surface for several hours before rinsing it off.

**2** Improve heating and ventilation in rooms affected by mould.

**3** Round window frames, fill any roughness in the frame surface or the bedding putty that could harbour spores, and paint right up to the glass surface. Wipe away condensation when it occurs. Ideally, fit double-glazing at badly affected windows.

● See also CONDENSATION.

# MOULDINGS

Decorative timber mouldings such as door architraves and skirtings – and even the panelling on panelled doors – are a feature of many older houses; newer homes tend to have plain fittings. The drawback with these fittings is that regular redecoration often clogs up their fine detail; the only way to restore it is to strip away all the old paint back to bare wood.

**ACTION**

**1** If you intend to repaint your mouldings, you will find that the quickest and cheapest method is to use a blowlamp. Any slight charring that occurs will be covered by the new paint. Tackle the intricate parts of the moulding first so that the old paint on the wood surrounding them will provide some protection against charring. Use a combination shavehook to reach into awkward corners, and a penknife or similar tool to dislodge the most stubborn and hard-to-reach bits. Sand the surface thoroughly when it has been stripped.

**2** If you prefer to use a chemical stripper in order to stain or varnish the stripped wood afterwards, use either a liquid stripper or the newer blanket-type product. With the former you will have to use steel wool to work the stripper into deep detail; wear rubber gloves to protect your hands. With the blanket type you should be able to peel off several layers of paint at once, although with heavily clogged mouldings a second or third application may be needed locally. Follow the manufacturer's instructions about surface preparation prior to redecoration.

See also CORNICES and STRIPPING PAINT.

## NAILS

Nails are probably the most widely used fixing for all sorts of practical jobs. To get the best results, there are several tips worth knowing.

**ACTION**

**1** When you are fixing two pieces of wood together, nail through the thinner piece into the thicker one. In general terms, use a nail at least two-and-a-half times as long as the thickness of the wood you are fixing.

**2** When driving small pins, use the wedge-shaped pein on your pin hammer to tap them in, or else push the pin through some thin card and use that as a holder until the pin is almost fully driven.

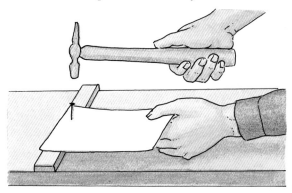

## NAILS

**3** When driving nails near the end of a piece of wood, do not position them all in a line or the grain will split. One way of avoiding this on narrow pieces is to leave a protruding 'horn' on the end, then cut it off when the nails have been driven.

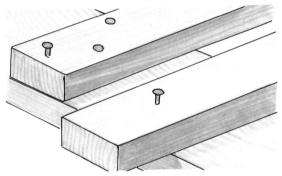

**4** If you drive nails flush with the wood, you will bruise it with the hammer. Avoid this by using a nail punch to drive the nail the last 1mm or 2mm ($\frac{1}{12}$in) – and to punch it below the surface if you want to hide the nail heads with stopping.

● See also FIXINGS and SCREWS.

## OVERFLOWS

To guard against water overflowing from baths, basins, sinks and cisterns if taps are left on or ballvalves malfunction, all these appliances have provision for water to escape via an overflow pipe. In bathroom and kitchen equipment, there is an overflow near the rim of the appliance that carries surplus water to the waste pipe below the plug; in cisterns, an overflow pipe is fitted above the water level and runs to the outside of the house, where it will discharge the water if the level rises too high in the cistern. For obvious reasons, such an overflow pipe should have a larger diameter than the feed pipe to the cistern; if the ballvalve does jam open, water can then flow out faster than it is flowing in.

**ACTION**

**1** Bath, basin and sink overflows may become blocked by scum, hair and grease. Test the overflow occasionally by filling the appliance above the overflow level to see if it runs away easily; the overflow should be able to cope if both taps are left running. If it cannot cope, clear it.

**2** If you notice a cistern overflow pipe dripping, either the ballvalve is jammed open or the ballvalve float is punctured and full of water. If the float is punctured, unscrew it from the float arm, empty it, tie a plastic bag over the float and reattach it. This is only a temporary repair; buy and fit a new plastic float at the earliest opportunity.

● See also BALLVALVES, BASINS, BLOCKAGES, CISTERNS, DOWNPIPES and GUTTERS.

## PAINTWORK

When you are redecorating, much of the work will involve putting a fresh coat of paint on already-painted walls and woodwork. You may be tempted to go for a quick cover-up by slapping paint directly over the existing surfaces, but you will get better results if you prepare the surface of the paintwork properly before you start redecoration.

**ACTION**

**1** Wash walls down with a strong solution of household detergent or sugar soap. Lay dustsheets to catch the inevitable drips, and work from the bottom up so that dirty water from higher up the wall is running down a wet surface and will not leave streaks. Rinse down thoroughly and leave to dry. In old houses the walls may have been painted with distemper, which will have to be removed if it is the non-washable type.

**2** Ceilings collect more grease and cigarette smoke stains than walls, and so should be thoroughly scrubbed. This is a messy job, best done wearing old clothes in a room stripped of all furniture. If it is not

## PAINTWORK

done, however, staining will soon show through the new coat of paint.

**3** Wash down paintwork in the same way as walls. Then sand over the entire surface with wet-and-dry abrasive paper, used wet, to flatten the gloss and provide a good key for the next coat of paint. This treatment will also remove any nibs and dust specks left over from previous repainting that could spoil the new finish. Rinse out the abrasive paper at intervals, and wipe down the paintwork with a clean damp cloth when you have finished the sanding.

See also DISTEMPER.

## PIPEWORK

Most homes have a certain amount of pipework on show: mostly pipe runs to radiators and clusters of pipes running up walls to and from boilers and hot tanks. It is a good idea to disguise or conceal such pipework if possible, as long as it remains accessible for repairs in the event of a leak or other problem.

**ACTION**

**1** The simplest way of disguising single pipes is to decorate them with the same colour paint as the surface they cross. Use gloss paint, not emulsion; you can obtain gloss paint to match most emulsion shades of the same brand. Simply degrease the pipework with white spirit, key it lightly by rubbing with emery paper and apply two coats of paint directly to the pipework (except iron pipe, which should be primed first).

**2** Groups of pipes can be boxed in with timber battens and plywood or hardboard panels. Make up a simple box-like structure big enough to enclose the pipes, and screw it to battens fixed to the wall so you can remove it easily if necessary. The boxing can be painted or papered to match the remaining decorations in the room so as to make it look less conspicuous.

See also BURSTS, FREEZE-UPS, LEAKS and METAL.

68

## PLASTER

Plaster is prone to accidental damage by carelessly moved furniture and the like, but can be patched easily and effectively if you know the right technique. External corners are particularly vulnerable to knocks.

### ACTION

1 To patch a small hole in plaster, use plaster or interior filler. Brush out loose debris, wet the hole and then use a filling knife to fill the hole slightly proud of the surrounding surface. When the repair has set, sand it down flush.

2 To patch a larger hole, strip the loose plaster back to bare masonry, and make sure the edges of the hole are sound by tapping them. Remove any unsound areas. Then dampen the wall and apply a coat of browning plaster to the masonry within the hole. Fill it to just below the surrounding surface, cross-hatch the surface with light strokes of the corner of your float and leave to harden. Then skim on a coat of finishing plaster flush with the surrounding surface, drawing a long batten over the patch to level it before polishing it up with a damp steel float.

3 To patch a corner, remove any loose plaster as in step 2. Then pin a batten to one face of the corner so its edge is level with the plaster surface on the adjacent wall and plaster that side of the corner first as in step 2 (base coat only). When the first area has hardened, remove the batten carefully and fix it to the plastered face so you can patch the second face. Finish off with a skim coat of finishing plaster on both faces, rounding off the corner slightly.

● See also CRACKS IN WALLS AND CEILINGS and LATH-AND-PLASTER.

## PLASTERBOARD

Plasterboard is a very versatile building material that is now used almost exclusively to cover ceilings and many wall surfaces in homes of all types. It consists of a plaster core covered on each side by stout paper, and is fixed to timber joists or studs with special galvanized plasterboard nails. It is made in two common thicknesses: 9mm (⅜in) and 12mm (½in). The thinner one needs supports at a maximum of 450mm (18in) centres, the thicker one at up to 600mm (2ft) centres. Where the joints between boards are to be taped, tapered-edge boards are used. If the surface is to be painted rather than papered, the board is fixed with its white face outermost. The commonest problem with plasterboard walls and ceilings is patching holes.

**ACTION**

**1** To patch a small hole in a plasterboard, cut away the jagged edges of the hole with a sharp knife, and brush out any loose plaster core material.

**2** Trim an offcut of plasterboard about 25mm (1in) wider than the hole in one dimension, narrow enough to pass through it in the other dimension. Bore a hole in the centre of the piece and thread a piece of knotted string through it.

**3** Butter some plaster or filler on to the ends of the piece on the opposite face to the knot in the string, poke it in through the hole and use the string to pull the patch back against the inner face of the plaster-

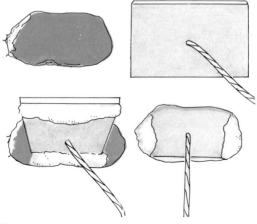

board. The plaster or filler will stick it in place. When it has set hard, cut off the string.

**4** Fill the recess that is left with plaster or filler.

## PLUGS

Plugs are the vital link between all electrical appliances and the mains supply. In older homes, round-pin plugs and sockets of different sizes may still be found, but the majority of houses now have standard three-pin plugs with rectangular pins that fit into a matching standard 13-amp socket outlet. Wiring your plugs up properly ensures safe electrical contact every time you plug in an appliance.

**ACTION**

**1** Open the plug and lay the flex loosely in position to measure the distance between the cord grip and the furthest terminal. Mark the flex sheath and cut it away carefully with a sharp knife back to the mark. Take care not to cut the insulation on the inner cores as you do this.

**2** Use wire strippers to remove about 12mm (½in) of insulation from each core. Take care not to cut through any of the core strands, then twist the strands neatly together.

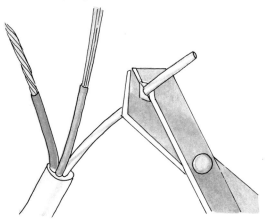

**3** Connect each core to its appropriate terminal. With the inside of the plug facing you, take the brown (live) core to the right terminal, the blue (neutral) core to the bottom left terminal, and the green/yellow core (absent on two-core flex) to the top earth terminal (the one with the longer pin). With stud terminals, wind the core round the stud in a clockwise direction and fit the stud; with pillar terminals double the strands over and insert them in the hole before tightening down the top screw. Make sure that the core insulation reaches right to the terminals, and that no loose strands are visible.

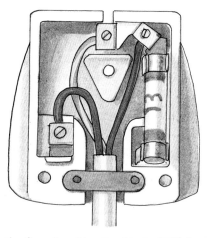

**4** Lay the flex sheathing in the cord grip and make sure it is held securely. The cores should have a little slack on them.

**5** Press in the plug fuse: a 3A (amp) one for appliances rated up to 750 watts and a 13A fuse for all other appliances and colour televisions.

**6** Replace the plug cover.

ALWAYS replace a damaged plug; it is very unsafe just to tape up cracks and hope for the best. NEVER replace the fuse with any other metallic object; you could kill someone. CHECK the cord grip and the connections within all plugs fitted to portable appliances at least once a year; set aside an afternoon for

the job, and remake any poor or loose connections.
See also ELECTRICITY, FLEX and FUSES.

## PLUMBING

Make sure you know your plumbing system: where all the pipes go, which pipe is which and, most importantly, where stoptaps are fitted. Knowing where these are means you can turn off the water supply in an emergency, and drain parts of the system for maintenance and repair work. Keep a simple plumbing tool kit handy for emergencies.
See also AIRLOCKS, BALLVALVES, BASINS, BATHS, BLOCKAGES, BURSTS, CISTERNS, FREEZE-UPS, LEAKS, OVERFLOWS, PIPES, RADIATORS, SHOWERS, SINKS, TAPS, WASHERS and WCs.

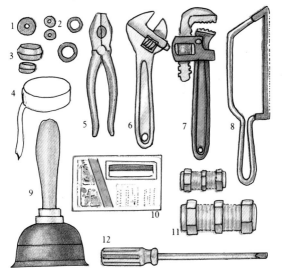

1 TAP WASHERS, 2 O-RINGS, 3 OLIVES 4 PTFE TAPE, 5 PLIERS,
6 ADJUSTABLE SPANNER 7 WRENCH, 8 JUNIOR HACKSAW,
9 PLUNGER, 10 TWO-PART EPOXY REPAIR PUTTY, 11 15 mm
AND 22 mm COMPRESSION COUPLINGS 12 SCREWDRIVER

## POWER POINTS

Power points allow you to connect electrical appliances to the fixed wiring at convenient points around the house, by means of a plug attached to the appliance flex. Unfortunately, there never seem to be enough of them, and the tendency is to use adaptors in order to allow extra appliances to share the same power point. This is unsatisfactory, because there is quite a risk of overloading the circuit and causing an electrical fire. Furthermore, the weight of the adaptor and several plugs can weaken the contacts within the power socket, leading to sparking and overheating. It is far better to put in extra power points where they are needed, and the simplest way of doing this is to turn existing single sockets into double outlets.

**ACTION**

**1** Turn off the mains switch at the consumer unit or fuse box and remove the fuse controlling the circuit you want to work on. Put it in your pocket so that no one can replace it without your knowledge, and turn the power to other circuits back on. If you have MCBs instead of rewireable fuses, trip the circuit MCB to 'off' and put some tape over the switch to alert anyone trying to turn it on.

**2** Unscrew the faceplate of the single socket, and disconnect the cable cores. If several cores of one colour are twisted together, leave them as they are.

**3** If the socket has a flush mounting box, fit a new double (or triple) surface-mounting box over it. Remove a knockout from the back of the new box, thread the cable(s) through it and use the original faceplate fixing screws to mount the new box to the fixing lugs of the old one.

**4** Connect the cable cores to the terminals of the new double (or triple) socket faceplate; red (live) cores go to the terminal marked L, black (neutral) cores to the terminal marked N and earth cores (which should be covered by slip-on green/yellow PVC sleeving) to the terminal marked E or ⏚. Tighten the terminal screws fully.

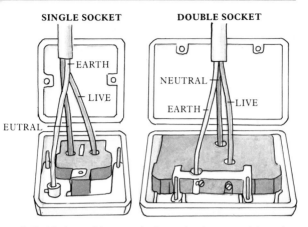

**SINGLE SOCKET**       **DOUBLE SOCKET**

EARTH

LIVE

EUTRAL

NEUTRAL

EARTH       LIVE

**5** Fold the cables neatly into the box, position the faceplate and screw it to the mounting box.

**6** Restore the power at the consumer unit and test that the new socket outlet is working properly. If it is not, check your connections carefully, and call an electrician if trouble persists.

● See also ELECTRICITY.

## PUTTY

Putty is used to secure panes of glass in wood and metal window frames. Use linseed oil putty in wood frames, metal casement putty with metal frames (some all-purpose putties are suitable for all windows). To prepare the putty for use, take a ball of it and roll it round in your hands to warm it up and blend in the oils evenly. If it is very oily, roll it out on some clean absorbent paper (newsprint will make the putty and your hands black). When you have puttied a window, paint over the new putty after two or three weeks to stop it cracking. You can store putty for a while if it is wrapped in plastic film to exclude all air, but it eventually hardens and becomes useless.

● See also GLASS and LEADED LIGHTS.

## RADIATORS

The most annoying problem with radiators is decorating behind them, especially if you are trying to remove old wallcoverings. The easiest solution is to remove the radiator, redecorate and replace the radiator afterwards.

**ACTION**

**1** Close the handwheel valve at one end of the radiator fully.

**2** Use a screwdriver to remove the cap from the lockshield valve at the other end, and then use pliers or a small spanner to close the lockshield valve itself by turning the spindle clockwise. Note how many turns this takes.

**3** Protect floorcoverings with polythene sheeting, and place a shallow bowl or tray under each valve, ready to catch the water from the radiator.

**4** Use an adjustable spanner to loosen the lock nuts attaching the valves to the radiator. Take care not to force them, or you may bend and split the pipe tails beneath each valve, with potentially messy consequences. Penetrating oil may help loosen stubborn nuts. Do not undo them fully yet.

**5** Use a spirit level to see if the radiator slopes slightly one way or the other. If it does, loosen the nut at the downhill end, and hold your bowl under the valve to catch the water as it runs out. It will probably be mixed with black sludge, the product of corrosion in the system.

**6** Once the water is trickling out, open the vent at the top of the radiator with a bleed key to speed up the process. When the flow slows to a trickle, undo the other lock nut, lift the radiator carefully off its brackets and tip out the last of the water. Set the radiator aside and mop up any drips.

**7** When you have redecorated, hang the radiator back on its brackets. Wrap some PTFE tape, or smear some plumber's jointing compound over the threaded end of each valve, and hand-tighten the locknuts. Then tighten them fully with a spanner.

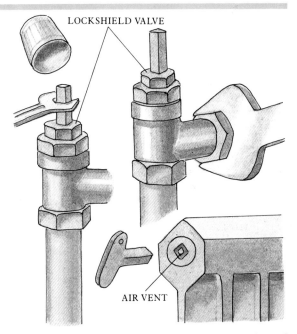

LOCKSHIELD VALVE

AIR VENT

**8** Open the lockshield valve by the same number of turns taken to close it (see step 2), and open the handwheel valve too. This will allow the radiator to fill with water from the header tank in the loft.
**9** Keep the vent open as the radiator fills, but be ready to close it as soon as water begins to flow.
**10** Check the locknut connections for leaks, and tighten the nuts slightly if necessary.

## ROT

Essentially, there are two kinds of rot: dry rot and wet rot. Dry rot is the more serious for, although the fungus initially develops in damp conditions, it then spreads into adjacent timber and masonry and can travel from room to room. Often, by the time dry rot is discovered, it has become well established and the drastic treatment required is best left to experts.

## ROT

Wet rot, however, only spreads as far as the damp itself and is therefore more easily dealt with. Even in a well-maintained house, wet rot is quite common: vulnerable points include window sills and glazing bars, timber cladding and the foot of outside door frames. The fungus's progress is often concealed under paintwork, and is only noticed during redecoration. If the timber is badly rotted, there is little alternative but to cut out the rotten wood and joint in new timber. However, milder attacks can be treated with a proprietary wood repair kit.

**ACTION**

**1** Scrape off all old paint from the affected area.

**2** Remove all loose fibres and crumbly wood.

**3** Brush on wood hardener, following the manufacturer's instructions carefully.

**4** Mix up the filler paste according to instructions and fill any cracks or holes. Allow to harden fully.

**5** Drill holes in surrounding timber, insert preservative pellets and fill holes with filler paste.

**6** Sand surfaces smooth and redecorate with primer, undercoat and top coat.

● See also CONDENSATION, DAMP and SILLS.

## RUST

If left untreated, rust will eventually eat its way through the surface it is attacking, causing problems like leaks in radiators, holes in gutters and damaged galvanized roofs. Treatment is relatively simple if tackled early on, and will enable the surfaces to be redecorated successfully.

**ACTION**

**1** Remove as much rust as possible from the affected surface using a scraper or wire brush.

**2** Brush on proprietary rust remover, following the manufacturer's instructions carefully.

**3** Neutralize or rinse the surface if instructed.

**4** Apply the appropriate primer, then undercoat and top coat to protect the surface.

5 Treat rust spots promptly when they occur on metalwork so that small outbreaks do not spread.
- See also METAL and WROUGHT IRON.

## SASH WINDOWS

The commonest problem with sash windows is broken sash cords. If one breaks, the window will jam and be almost impossible to open or close. Since the sashes have to be removed to fit a new cord, it makes sense to replace all of them at the same time; otherwise another old cord may break in the near future, and the whole job will have to be done again.

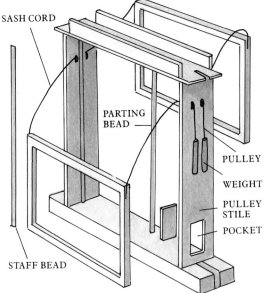

SASH CORD

PARTING BEAD

PULLEY

WEIGHT

PULLEY STILE

POCKET

STAFF BEAD

**ACTION**
1 Prise off the staff beads with a chisel and open up the pocket pieces at each side of the frame. Retrieve the weight from the side where the cord is broken, and wedge up the inner sash so you can pull the weight from the other side and cut its cord.
2 Lower the inner sash and lift it out. Prise out the

tacks holding the sash cord to the sides of the sash.

**3** Prise off the parting bead between the sashes, wedge up the outer sash, cut off the weights and lift the sash down.

**4** Rehang the outer sash first. Tie a length of string to one end of the new sash cord and attach a small weight to the end of the string, small enough to pass over the pulley.

**5** Pass the weight over the outer pulley, let it drop inside the weight compartment, retrieve it and use it to pull the sash cord over the pulley. Attach the weight. Repeat the process at the other side.

**6** Haul up each weight until it hangs just below the pulley, and pin the cord temporarily in place alongside the parting bead groove. Let it hang down towards the pocket, and cut the cord about 50mm (2in) above the top of the pocket.

**7** Hold the outer sash in place in the frame, resting it on the sill, and attach the cords to the sides of the sash with tacks. Push the sash up to its closed position and check that the weights drop almost to the bottom of each weight compartment.

**8** Replace the parting bead, and repeat the procedure for the inner sash. Here the weights will be in the top position when the sash is closed, and will drop as it is opened. Finally, replace the pocket pieces and the staff bead.

# SCRATCHES

When wooden furniture is scratched or scarred – for example, by a burning cigarette – it is often possible to make a localized cosmetic repair job that avoids the need for the piece to be completely stripped and refinished.

**ACTION**

**1** If the scratch only affects the finish, try disguising it by rubbing in proprietary scratch-cover polish or wax shoe polish of an appropriate shade.

**2** With a deeper scrape, which exposes bare wood of a different colour to the surrounding wood, try touching up the colour with diluted wood stain or poster paint. Then brush on diluted varnish with an artist's brush, applying several coats until the repair stands proud of the surface. Allow to harden, sand smooth with fine glasspaper and then polish.

**3** With cigarette burns, use a sharp knife to scrape away the finish and any charred wood. Sand the bare wood with glasspaper, then stain and apply layers of varnish to build up the repair. Sand and polish as in step 2. Fill deep holes with coloured wax.

See also LAMINATES.

## SCREWS

When you buy screws, you should give a detailed specification to be sure of getting the right screw. You have to include the gauge (a measure of the screw's diameter: the smaller the number the slimmer the screw); the length; the head style (countersunk, raised countersunk, round, etc.); the slot type (slotted, Pozidriv, etc.); the material (steel, brass, etc.) and the finish – if a special colour or plating is required. One of the commonest problems with screws is removing them, especially if they are stuck or the head is damaged.

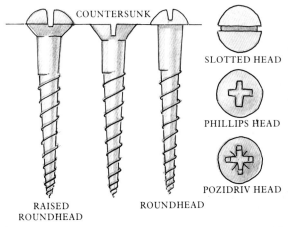

COUNTERSUNK

SLOTTED HEAD

PHILLIPS HEAD

POZIDRIV HEAD

RAISED ROUNDHEAD

ROUNDHEAD

# SCREWS

## ACTION

**1** Use a screwdriver with a tip that matches the slot length and thickness. If it will not move with reasonable pressure, do not force it or you may damage the slot. Try using a brace and screwdriver bit for greater leverage.

**2** If this fails, hold the screwdriver at a slight angle in the slot and strike the handle with a hammer or mallet. This may break the wood's grip on the screw thread and allow it to be turned.

**3** If this fails, try heating the head of the screw for a short while with a hot soldering iron. This may loosen the screw by causing it to expand, and so make it easy to withdraw when it has cooled.

**4** If all else fails, or if the screw head is badly damaged, you will have to drill it out using a twist drill in a hand or electric drill. Work at slow speed until you reach the shank of the screw and you can release whatever it is fixing. Leave the body of the screw in the wood.

**5** When driving screws, always make a pilot hole with a bradawl or twist drill, and also a clearance hole to allow the screw shank to enter the wood without binding. Dipping the screw in a little wax or soap will make it easier to withdraw in future.

See also FIXINGS.


# SHELVES

Unless shelves are supported by brackets at regular intervals, they will sag, especially if heavily laden. If you are using 12mm (½in) thick chipboard, or veneered or plastic-coated chipboard, fit brackets at 450mm (18in) centres for shelves carrying books and the like, at 600mm (2ft) centres for lighter loads. With 19mm (¾in) chipboard or 12mm (½in) plywood, fix brackets at 600mm (2ft) centres for heavy loads, at 750mm (2ft 6in) centres for lighter loads. Fix individual brackets using a spirit level; if you are putting up adjustable shelving systems a slightly different technique is needed.

ACTION
1 Use a spirit level to mark a true horizontal line on the wall where the tops of the uprights will go.
2 Mark the upright spacings along this line.
3 Hold each upright up to the line, and mark the position of its topmost fixing screw on the wall. Drill and plug the hole and drive the screw partly home. Repeat for other uprights.
4 Check that the upright is hanging vertically. Then mark all the other fixing screw positions, swing the upright aside and drill and plug all the holes. Drive all the fixing screws. Repeat the process for the other uprights.
5 Slot the brackets into the uprights and lay the shelves in position. With some systems you can screw the shelves to the brackets for extra rigidity; attach the brackets and then place the shelves on the uprights.

  See also FIXINGS.

## SHOWERS

A common problem with showers of all types, particularly in hard-water areas, is scaling at the rose. This gradually blocks the holes, eventually reducing the water flow to a trickle.
ACTION
1 Dismantle the rose if possible so you can get at the inner surface of the rose plate itself.
2 Scrape or scrub off hard scale deposits from the inner surface of the rose, using a pin to clear blocked holes. Then reassemble the rose.
3 If you cannot open up the rose, try poking out all the holes with a pin to loosen the deposits. If the rose can be undone from the shower hose, shake out the loosened deposits, and hold the rose holes uppermost under running water to flush it out completely. Reconnect it to the shower hose.
4 If the rose still appears to be blocked, experiment by immersing it in an electric kettle filled with descaling compound (you can descale the kettle at the

same time). However, this treatment may affect plating on metal roses, and could soften plastic ones.

## SILLS

Timber window sills are particularly prone to damage from rot, especially if they are not carefully painted to stop moisture entering. Small localized areas of rot can be treated with a proprietary wood repair kit, but larger areas will have to be cut out and replaced.

**ACTION**

**1** Mark out a wedge-shaped section round the damaged area.

**2** Cut carefully along the angled lines across the grain, using a tenon saw or a powered jigsaw.

**3** Chisel along the grain to remove the rest of the rotten wood, and clean up the recess.

**4** Use a sliding bevel (or cut a paper template) to transfer the angles of the cut-out to the new timber section. Cut one end, then check the angle on the other before cutting it.

**5** Smear woodworking adhesive over the meeting surfaces, offer up the new section and drill and countersink holes in it to take the fixing screws. Screw it into place and wipe away excess adhesive.

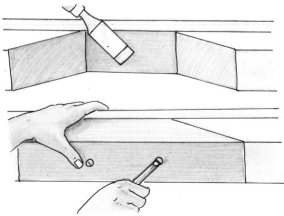

**6** Plane the new wood down carefully to match the existing sill profile (make sure the screw heads are well countersunk). Fill the screwholes, then prime and paint the new section.

See also CONDENSATION and ROT.

## SINKS

Kitchen sinks are extremely vulnerable to block-ages, caused by a build-up of food debris and grease. Fitting a waste disposal unit means that all food debris is liquidized before being flushed away, but blockages can still occur unless the trap and waste run is cleaned out regularly. Try to avoid emptying tea leaves and cooking oils down the sink waste; the two together can block a sink trap in next to no time.
**ACTION**
**1** Clean sink traps and wastes out every week by making up a strong solution of hot washing soda and pouring it into the trap. Leave for about an hour, then flush through with clean water.
**2** If a blockage does occur, you will have to dis-mantle the trap and remove blockage mechanically.

See also BASINS, BLOCKAGES, DRAINS and GULLIES.

## SKIRTING BOARDS

Gaps between the wall surface and the skirting board are unsightly and difficult to fill, especially on ground floors where the boards are often fixed to timber 'grounds' and so are unsupported behind the major part of each length; this means that if the skirting is kicked or knocked the plaster immedi-ately above it will crack away. Plaster or rigid filler will stop the gap for a while, but it will eventually fall out.
**ACTION**
**1** If the wall surface is painted directly on to plaster, fill the gap with a bead of non-setting mastic. If the

gap is wide, pack it first with soft rope or similar material to stop the mastic slumping into the gap. Then paint the mastic.

**2** If the wall surface is papered, repeat the process and paint the mastic to match the skirting board. When you redecorate, trim the new wallcovering so it is long enough to reach on to the top edge of the skirting board, and brush it carefully into the angle to conceal the crack.

• See also CRACKS IN WALLS AND CEILINGS and MASONRY.

## STAIRCASES

Staircases are complex pieces of joinery that are subject to constant wear. They generally stand up to this well, but may start to creak. The reason for this is a loosening of some of the components.

**ACTION**

**1** Cure squeaky treads and risers by injecting wood-working adhesive into the gaps between the treads and risers. Then drive screws down through the treads into the edges of the risers below.

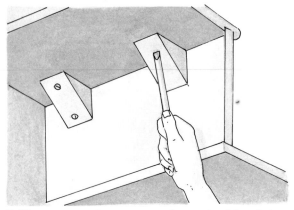

**2** If you can gain access to the underside of the staircase, glue and screw blocks of wood into the angles between treads and risers; also tap back any

wedges that have become loose where the treads meet the strings at the sides of the flight.
- See also FLOORS.

## STRIPPING PAINT

You can strip paint from woodwork in several ways: by scraping and sanding (slow and laborious), by using a blowlamp (quick and inexpensive, but will char the wood) or with a chemical paint stripper (efficient and leaves the wood with a natural grain and colour, but expensive). Which method you choose will depend on what you are stripping, how big an area is involved, and how you want to treat the newly-exposed surface.

**ACTION**

**1** If you are using a blowlamp, work from the bottom upwards, so the heat from the flame can rise and soften the paint above as you work. Play the flame back and forth over a small area at a time until the paint begins to soften and bubble; then scrape it off with a scraper or shavehook and deposit the hot scrapings in a tin, not in a plastic container. If you are stripping intricate mouldings, tackle them before you strip the surrounding areas to minimize charring.

**2** If you are using paint stripper, follow the manufacturer's instructions carefully. With methylene dichloride types, wear gloves and work in a well-ventilated atmosphere. Use an old brush to work the stripper well into the paint surface; when the paint has bubbled, scrape it off and transfer the sludge to a tin to prevent blobs falling on to the floor.
- See also CORNICES, DOORS and MOULDINGS.

## STRIPPING WALLCOVERINGS

There is often a temptation to hang a new wallcovering on top of an existing one, but this is seldom satisfactory because the paste used to hang the new wallcovering can soften the old adhesive and cause the existing paper to lift in unsightly bubbles. There may also be an adhesion problem. The only safe answer is to strip the old wallcovering completely.

**ACTION**

**1** Remove ordinary wallpapers by soaking them with warm water to which a little washing up liquid has been added. When the paper softens, soak it again and then scrape it off with a flat-bladed scraper. Do not use a filling knife: the blade is too flexible.

**2** Washable wallpapers and painted relief wallcoverings will not absorb water unless the surface is broken up first with a serrated scraper. This is a time-consuming process that can also damage the plaster; a more satisfactory and much simpler method is to use a steam wallpaper stripper, which can be hired by the day.

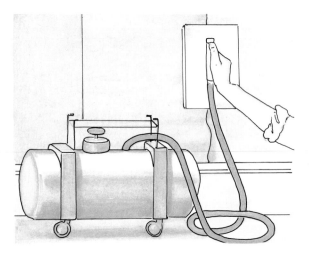

**3** Strip vinyls by peeling off the vinyl layer length by length; then soak and remove the backing paper as in step 1.

- See also ANAGLYPTA, CORK WALL TILES, HESSIAN, LINCRUSTA and LINING PAPER.

## TAPS

The flow of water through a tap is controlled by a spindle that rises and falls as the tap is turned on and off; the spindle lifts or lowers a rubber washer on to the water inlet within the body of the tap. If this washer becomes worn or compressed, the tap will drip – and will waste a surprisingly large amount of water. It is a simple matter to replace it.

**ACTION**

1 On a pillar tap, wrap the shroud in cloth to protect it and use a wrench to undo the shroud.

2 Loosen the grub screw holding the capstan head on the spindle.

3 Lift off the handle and shroud.

4 Cut off the water supply to the tap at the appropriate stopcock. Open the tap.

5 Undo the headgear with a spanner or wrench.

6 Pull out the washer and jumper unit, prise off the

old washer and press on a new one of the correct size
– ¾in for bath taps, ½in otherwise.

**7** Push the jumper unit back into place, refit the headgear and tighten with spanner or wrench.

**8** Replace the shroud and handle, close the tap and restore the water supply.

**9** On a modern shrouded-head tap, the handle may simply pull off to allow access to the headgear. If it does not, prise off the coloured hot/cold disc to reveal a grub screw which has to be loosened to release the handle. Proceed as for a pillar tap.

● See also BURSTS.

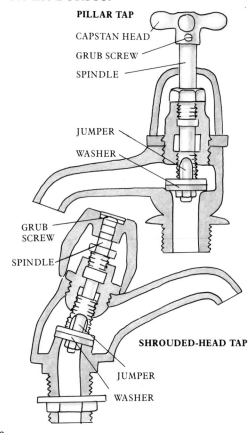

PILLAR TAP

CAPSTAN HEAD

GRUB SCREW

SPINDLE

JUMPER

WASHER

GRUB SCREW

SPINDLE

SHROUDED-HEAD TAP

JUMPER

WASHER

## TILES

See CERAMIC TILES, CORK FLOORS, CORK WALL TILES, EXPANDED POLYSTYRENE and MIRRORS.

## TIMBER

When you are buying timber, remember that the sizes are nominal ones, not actual ones. Sawn timber is 1mm or 2mm smaller in each cross dimension than the nominal size, and planed timber will be 3mm or more below the nominal size. So a piece of sawn wood that is nominally 50mm (2in) square will actually measure about 48mm square, while planed timber of the same nominal size may actually measure only 45mm or 46mm square. Timber is still sometimes sold by the linear foot (12in/305mm), but many timber merchants and other outlets use the metric foot of 300mm. So if you order 'six feet' of wood, you may get 6×300mm = 1800mm (5ft 10¾in); the difference could be critical.

**ACTION**

**1** When buying wood, check that the actual cross-section is the size you want. If you need an exact size, you will have to plane down sawn wood of the next available larger size.

**2** Watch out for the metric foot. If you need wood of an exact length, say so. You may have to buy an extra metric foot to get exactly the length you want.

See also CHAIRS, DOORS, DRAWERS, FLOORS, ROT and WOODWORM.

## TOOLS

Good tools are expensive, so it pays to look after them. Care in use, care in storage, regular sharpening and common sense will all help to make your tools last longer.

## TOOLS

### ACTION

**1** Use each tool only for its particular purpose: chisels are not screwdrivers and mallets will not drive nails.

**2** Do not store tools in a jumble. Hang them up in racks or with spring clips. Coil the flex of power tools neatly. Before you put bladed tools away, smear with petroleum jelly to prevent rusting and protect the blades with a guard.

**3** Sharpen tools such as chisels and planes regularly. Blunt tools cut badly and can cause accidents as they are forced through the wood.

**4** Handle all tools, especially bladed and power tools, with care. Keep your hands behind the cutting line of chisels and saws.

## VINYL FLOORS

Vinyl floorcoverings are extremely hardwearing, but can be damaged by sharp impact and by contact with hot objects. Such damage is best repaired by cutting out the affected area and inserting a patch.

### ACTION

**1** Obtain an offcut of the floorcovering (if no spare material was kept when the vinyl was originally laid, cut away a piece from under a fitted unit or other fixed furniture).

**2** Lay it over the damaged area, matching the pattern carefully, and cut through offcut and vinyl with a sharp handyman's knife.

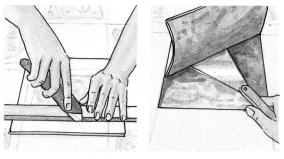

**3** Prise up the damaged portion of the vinyl. If it was stuck down, scrape away the old backing and adhesive. If it was not, lift the edges of the hole and brush flooring adhesive underneath them.

**4** Coat the back of the patch with flooring adhesive and lay it in place. Hammer it down over a block of wood to protect the vinyl. Wipe away any excess adhesive and then weight the repair overnight.

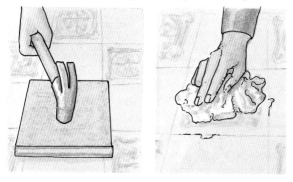

## WALLCOVERINGS

See ANAGLYPTA, BRICKWORK, CERAMIC TILES, CORK WALL TILES, DISTEMPER, HESSIAN, LINCRUSTA, LINING PAPER, MIRRORS, MOULD, PLASTER, RADIATORS and STRIPPING WALLCOVERINGS.

## WASHERS

See TAPS.

## WCs

A blocked WC is a plumbing problem that has to be solved on the spot. Unlike other appliances, you cannot gain access to the trap, so the blockage usually has to be tackled from above.

**ACTION**

**1** Use a 100mm (4in) diameter rubber plunger with a metal disc above the cup. The disc prevents the cup turning inside out as you work the plunger.

**2** Lower the plunger into the pan until the cup touches the sides.

**3** Plunge it up and down with short vigorous thrusts to force short surges of water into the bend and dislodge the blockage.

**4** When the blockage has been cleared, flush the cistern to refill the trap and wash away the remains of the blockage.

**5** If you cannot clear the blockage and the WC is on the ground floor, check the manhole on its drain run. You may be able to clear the blockage by rodding up the run from the manhole. However, this will not work if the blockage is in the short vertical section of pipe from the pan. In this case, you will have to call a plumber to clear the blockage with special flexible drain-clearing equipment.

● See also BLOCKAGES and DRAINS.

## WINDOWS

● See DOORS, DRAUGHTPROOFING, GLASS, HINGES, LEADED LIGHTS, MASONRY, PUTTY, ROT and SILLS.

## WIRING

● See BELLS, CABLE, ELECTRICITY, FLEX, FLUORESCENT LIGHTS, FUSES, LIGHTS, PLUGS and POWER POINTS.

## WOODBLOCK FLOORS

Properly laid, a woodblock floor will give years of service. However, individual blocks may become loose, or may be damaged in some way.

**ACTION**

**1** If the damage is fairly superficial, use glasspaper or a power sander to strip the surface finish and remove the scar or dent. Then refinish the block to match its surroundings: stain it first if the exposed wood is much paler, or bleach it if it is darker, than the existing colour.

**2** If a block is loose, lift it and scrape away any remains of old adhesive from underneath. Then brush in a little flooring adhesive and push the block into place, level with its neighbours. Add more adhesive if it sits too low, and sand it down if it is a little high (in this case you will have to wait until the adhesive is dry).

**3** If a block is badly damaged, use a chisel to prise it up, taking care not to damage its neighbours as you work. Scrape up old adhesive from the recess.

**4** Cut a new block of hardwood that matches the colour of the other blocks (you may be able to get some scrap wood from a timber merchant), check its fit in the recess and stick into place with flooring adhesive. Refinish it to match its neighbours.

## WOODWORM

The small holes left in furniture and structural timbers by woodworm are caused by the emerging beetle: the pest has spent its earliest years as a grub munching through the wood before hatching into an insect just below the surface and tunnelling its way out. Infestation is rarely severe enough to cause structural damage, but an attack can be particularly serious if it affects fine furniture.

**ACTION**

**1** Treat affected furniture by squirting aerosol woodworm killer into all the flight holes, and by polishing or varnishing all bare wood so that newly-laid eggs will be discouraged.

**2** Spray affected structural timber with woodworm killer, using a low-pressure spray unit. Clear all areas of furniture and other effects before treatment, and wear goggles and a mask as you work. Alternatively, call in professionals to carry out the work – usually essential if treatment is called for by a building society, since the firm will give a guarantee.

## WROUGHT IRON

Decorative wrought ironwork rusts rapidly if it is not well painted, and can eventually corrode completely. Since restoration work is tedious, it is best to maintain ironwork regularly to avoid problems.

**ACTION**

**1** If rust is extensive, strip all old paint back to bare metal with a blowlamp or chemical stripper.

**2** Remove rust with a wire brush or chemical rust remover.

**3** Degrease the surface with white spirit, and then treat with red lead or calcium plumbate primer (outdoors), or with zinc chromate primer (indoors: it is lead-free). Leave to dry. Apply a second coat.

**4** Finish off with undercoat and topcoat.

See also METAL and RUST.